GRADUATE EDUCATION

GRADUATE EDUCATION:

A CRITIQUE AND A PROGRAM

OLIVER C. *ronwell* CARMICHAEL

former President
THE CARNEGIE FOUNDATION
FOR THE ADVANCEMENT OF TEACHING

HARPER & BROTHERS
Publishers, New York

CONTENTS

Preface

During the past two years I have visited some forty universities in search of the facts about graduate education. In most institutions I have talked with the presidents and graduate deans. In many I have interviewed the undergraduate deans, department heads, registrars, and other members of the teaching staff. I am deeply indebted to all those witnesses, not only for the information they furnished but also for the views on the status and needs of graduate education. While they have been most helpful, they, of course, are in no way responsible for the views expressed in this report.

In addition to the recent intensive study of the problems and prospects of graduate education, I served as a graduate dean for two years and as administrative head of two universities that had graduate schools for a total of twelve years. Moreover, as president of the Carnegie Foundation for the Advancement of Teaching for eight years, I had considerable experience working with graduate deans and their faculties.

Thus, the conclusions reached and the recommendations set forth in this volume are based upon a broad background of experience, as well as upon recent research which was supported by the Fund for the Advancement of Education.

I owe a special debt of gratitude to Mr. Alvin C. Eurich and Mr. Clarence Faust, of the Fund for the Advancement of Education, not only for their generous support of the project but also for their interest and encouragement. In addition to the support and general encouragement, Mr. Eurich took time out of a busy schedule to read much of the original draft and to submit valuable comments and suggestions for the improvement of the text. Though most grateful to the officials of the Fund for their help and encouragement, I hasten to add that neither the Fund nor its officers are responsible for the views expressed, the conclusions reached, or the recommendations made. This is emphasized by the author since he recognizes that some of the views and criticisms of existing policies and practices are not commonly accepted and, hence, are unlikely to meet with general approval.

I am fully aware that the recommendation respecting the reorganization of the graduate school has been debated for years and that many deans of graduate schools have expressed opposition to it. Despite this fact, I have been forced to the conclusion, after a long and intensive study of the matter, that critical problems of graduate education can never be solved without reorganization. I have found, therefore, no alternative to making a specific recommendation that graduate schools be given greater autonomy, greater responsibility, and greater authority. Under the present organization basic reforms are not possible. This apparently accounts for the fact that while all other divisions of the university have undergone a variety of changes and improvements, the graduate school has remained static.

Previous study reports have included criticisms and recommendations, but both the criticisms and recommendations have dealt with relatively minor aspects of existing practices or policies. None have suggested a new approach, a comprehensive program that involved basic changes. This report includes two elements, an appraisal and a program.

The second part suggests not only a rather specific program for the master's and Ph.D. degrees, but a plan for the upper two college years for those deemed capable of graduate work. The three-years master's degree, outlined in Chapter 8, contemplates the introduction of the university idea of scholarship in the third year of college for gifted students, including some research, writing and independent reading. This extra work is designed as preparation for graduate work, thus making it easier for the student to adjust to graduate school requirements.

The program actually involves the first two years of college for the talented student, through the provision that a *pregraduate* group be formed which would be similar to the premedical and prelaw groups already common in colleges. In a sense, then, the recommendations contemplate a single integrated program of higher education covering seven years, from high school graduation to the Ph.D. degree. This could, of course, apply only to the upper 15 to 20 per cent in most institutions, for the others would not usually be interested in doing advanced work.

Perhaps it should also be said that the details of the program in many cases are included as a means of clarifying the general scheme; they are not considered important for any other reason. In other words, there is nothing inflexible about them. A wide variation in detail is possible without affecting the achievement of the objectives.

An important change embodied in the program provides for full-time faculty members who will have primary responsibility for graduate education and the authority to carry out plans formulated by the graduate school. Such a group could make a more thorough study of the needs, and how best to meet them, in a given institution than any single individual making a general study of the subject. It is for this reason that the details of the plan are not considered inflexible.

Part 1   *A CRITIQUE*

Introduction

No other phase of higher education has been subject to the critical scrutiny that graduate schools have undergone in the past few years. Institutional, regional, and national studies have been made. Every facet of research and graduate work has been probed. The graduate deans, individually and collectively, have debated the age-old issues: the deplorable state of the M.A., the failure of recruiting programs, the inordinate lag between the B.A. and the Ph.D., the lack of articulation between undergraduate and graduate work, the controversy over the language requirement, the unsatisfactory situation with respect to the qualifiying and final examinations, the nature and length of the dissertation, the structure and organization of graduate schools, and so on ad infinitum.

Despite all the studies, reports, discussions, debates, and criticisms, little progress has been made toward the solution of the problems which, by unanimous agreement, are recognized as serious stumbling blocks, affecting adversely all phases of education. No new issues have appeared, and no fresh approaches have been suggested for the resolution of the old ones. Many have been more sharply defined, and all have been emphasized, more in recent years than previously, but no one has proposed a new program as a means of solving these problems. It is a major purpose of this study to outline such a program.

It is not a historical study. Excellent background studies already exist. It is not a statistical study. Bernard Berelson, Hans Rosenhaupt, and Dean Peter Elder of Harvard have recently provided a wealth of statistical data not only about what takes place in graduate schools but what administrations, faculties, and graduate students think about the status of graduate education in American universities. It is not merely a factual study of the policies and practices of graduate schools and faculties, nor primarily a critical study, though policies, procedures, and results are appraised with candor. The major concern is to suggest a plan that, it is hoped, will indicate possible solutions to some of the chief problems that have long been recognized but about which little or nothing has been done.

Some of the recommendations may appear radical, unworkable, or even heretical. I am aware of the manifold difficulties involved in achieving basic changes in university education at any level, and particularly in the graduate school. The fact that graduate school policies and procedures have changed less than those of the college or of any of the professional schools is the evidence. While this seems a strange phenomenon, the background and reasons for it may emerge as we consider the structure and operation of the graduate education program.

The attempt here is to evaluate not only practices and procedures but the program and spirit of the graduate school, the validity of some of its premises, the confusion that exists in the over-all picture and in individual institutional procedures. The lack of consistency in institutional practices that permits different standards in the different departments will be examined. In some institutions the time lag between the B.A. and the Ph.D. in English, for instance, is almost twice as great as it is in some other departments. An individual professor may hold up the degree of a capable student several years without informing the rest of the graduate faculty or the dean. The matter of attrition and the time lag between the B.A. and the Ph.D. are considered in some detail.

The fact that usually the graduate dean has no real authority is common knowledge. A decision that he and the graduate council make can be thwarted by a single undergraduate department, if the head is not in agreement with it: this sometimes happens in the best of our graduate schools. The question of whether such a situation can be justified is raised in view of the strategic role of the graduate school in American higher education. The present organization and practices may have been reasonably satisfactory when graduate enrollments were small, but now, with more than three hundred thousand enrollees each year, are they adequate? Why should graduate school proposals for change require unanimous agreement when other educational policy matters require only a majority vote?

Some have suggested that the graduate dean should have a budget, as do all other deans of the university; others oppose it vigorously. This anomalous situation is reviewed in detail with some examination of the arguments pro and con. There may be a compromise arrangement which would meet the approval of both sides. The seriousness of the situation is illustrated by the practice, which prevails in some cases at least, of an institution's making a major appointment on the recommendation of the undergraduate dean without the approval of his counterpart in the graduate school, though the appointee is expected to be a member of the graduate faculty. This practice may no longer obtain in the stronger universities, but should not a policy that permits such a practice be discontinued?

Under the prevailing system the debates in graduate councils and faculties, as well as in dean's conferences, have appeared unrealistic. At times it has seemed, that the failure to reach decisions was due partly to the realization on the part of those present that, since they could not commit their institutions, no clear-cut action was necessary.

The relationship of the graduate faculty member to the school is also discussed. He not only is a part-time worker in graduate education but owes his first allegiance to the undergraduate or professional school department. This means that no one in the university considers graduate education a primary responsibility except the dean, and even he usually owes his position in the university to the department of which he is a member.

The question is posed whether authority to make binding decisions may not be essential to the development of a fully effective graduate program. The graduate school enrollment is now substantially larger than the entire college and university enrollments were in 1900. One wonders what the state of higher education in the United States would be today if college faculties in the past sixty years had been part-time teachers and had had no more authority to make decisions and carry them out than the present graduate faculties have.

Other substantive questions are raised. What is the nature of the graduate instruction and research now conducted by graduate schools? Do they meet current needs? Is there a problem of adjusting to the modern emphasis upon science and technology? How can the difficulty of meshing the scientific and technological program with university tradition be met? These basic and relevant questions have not been given adequate attention in discussions of higher education.

With the admission of science and technology to university curriculums a century ago, a new approach, the scientific method, was introduced. It was hailed as the accepted method in the search for truth in all areas. Its limitations in the field of the humanities and in their offspring, the social sciences, have not yet been fully recognized. This fundamental problem is discussed at length in several chapters.

Another related factor in humanistic-social studies research, which has never been adequately taken into consideration, is that more than facts are involved. Values, which are less clearly defined than objective facts, play an essential role. Emotional overtones, which defy analysis or description, are involved in great literature, great painting, or great music. In other words, something more than scientific analysis or flawless logic is required. Depth of appreciation and inspiration should be the result of deep study of masterpieces of thought and expression. A dissertation that reported the results of such study and contemplation of a masterpiece might be more appropriate than a factual report on its style or on its historical setting or on any literary allusions in it. Creative expression on the part of the student, as well as extension of factual knowledge, should be the goal of humanistic-social studies research.

Another aim of graduate education, included in this study, is preparation for college and university teaching. The age-old controversy about whether research and graduate work fit or unfit one for teaching in an arts college is reviewed. In a recent article, *The Graduate School and the Decline of Liberal Education,* Earl McGrath maintains that the graduate schools are responsible for a disastrous decline in the effectiveness of the college and in liberal education in general. He ascribes this decline to the fact that specialized research and liberal education are antithetical. He suggests that the college, which is an institution copied from the English, was never meant to be joined with the graduate school, which reflects the German philosophy of education.

This thesis is examined in some detail in the light of the new type of research proposed for the humanities and social sciences. Among the conclusions reached are: (1) that the graduate schools are the only training agencies for college teachers and, hence, are indispensable to our system of education; (2) that research of the right kind is not only not harmful but essential to liberal education; and (3) that a different focus in the humanistic-social studies fields should result in converting the graduate schools into a source of great strength to the arts colleges.

Another criticism of the graduate school is based on the fact that so few doctoral graduates continue productive research after the dissertation is approved and the degree granted. This indicates that though research is a major requirement for advanced degrees, it does not constitute a major activity of the majority of Ph.D. holders. In short, the complaint is that the research training is ineffective, as judged by the record, in producing research scholars. Thus, graduate education is blamed for emphasizing research and spoiling good teachers and, at the same time, for not producing scholars despite the great emphasis upon scholarly research.

Both these points of view are examined in the light of the

fact that whatever the weaknesses of graduate schools, they have grown more rapidly than colleges, which has given rise to the notion that they are operating satisfactorily. It is pointed out that growth is no criterion, that the need for advanced training is so overwhelming that these schools may have expanded despite their defects and not on account of their virtues.

Notwithstanding its fantastic growth, graduate work falls far short of meeting current demands. The reasons for this are examined in detail. It is pointed out particularly that the increase in the number of Ph.D.'s may not mean that the need for more college teachers is being met, for the majority of Ph.D. degrees now being given are in fields that are not related to liberal education. It has been recognized for some years that the master's degree no longer indicates basic scholarship, that it may be a fifth year of undergraduate work, a consolation degree, a professional degree, or a scholarly degree requiring, in some instances, two years beyond the B.A. What is not generally recognized is that there is probably as much variation in the doctor's degrees awarded as in the master's degrees.

For example, many Ph.D.'s are now granted for research in agriculture, engineering, business administration, teacher education, and other professional fields which do not qualify the holder to teach in a college. In recent years the majority of doctorates have been granted in these fields. Few educators realize the extent to which this is true, and the general public is unaware of it. The Ph.D. is no longer awarded primarily for research in the humanities, social sciences, or the natural sciences. Failure to recognize this fact may be responsible for the complacency, in some quarters, with respect to the state of graduate education.

The conclusion that there is no crisis in graduate education, only a minor problem, is critically examined. This view appears to stem, in part at least, from the failure to analyze in detail the character of the research for which the advanced degree is now being awarded, and to realize the drastic relative decline in the number of Ph.D.'s in the basic arts college subjects, judging by the list in recent volumes of *Dissertation Abstracts*. To read with care one of these volumes leaves one depressed over the state of American higher learning. In support of that feeling, a series of dissertation subjects is listed, in the hope that it may result in arousing graduate faculties to the realization that a new look at our graduate programs is needed.

It is not pleasant for me, a veteran laborer in the higher educational vineyard, to find fault with what is going on in the universities. But if discussing with complete frankness the defects that have appeared in the course of the study proves helpful in any way, the risk involved will be worth while. It is in this spirit that I have been critical. The hope of stirring up a new sense of the opportunity of graduate education, and of suggesting certain steps that might be helpful in strengthening the program, has been my purpose.

In addition to the strictures on the organization, curriculum, methods, and procedures of graduate education, a series of internal problems is listed. Among these are recruitment for graduate study, the articulation of undergraduate with graduate education, a clearer definition of what is expected of the student who comes up for the qualifying examination and of his preparation for it, the amount of course work required beyond the master's degree, the foreign language examinations, the need for developing a morale for college teaching as a profession, and the means of tightening up the program so that one may count on the Ph.D. as surely as the medical student counts on the M.D. degree if he does his part.

The summary of criticisms in Chapter X is an attempt to put together in concise form the various aspects of the graduate program that have been discussed and criticized for many years. Though the chapter involves repetition, it has nevertheless seemed important to bring together in one statement the central features of graduate education that have seemed least satisfactory. In this way a profile of the problems can be seen. It serves also as a kind of summary of Part 1.

As already suggested, the second part, which deals with a

proposed new program, represents an effort to be constructive. In too many instances criticisms of graduate education stop short of providing a plan for over-all improvement. The goal of this effort is to sketch in broad outlines, and yet concretely, a plan of organization and operation of graduate work that is designed to meet, at least partially, many of the criticisms detailed in the first part. Obviously there will not be general agreement on details, but if the main outlines of the plan are accepted as sound, it might serve as a basis for beginning a reorganization of higher education that would strengthen both the college and the graduate school and would provide a more coherent and integrated program of post-high school education than the one that now prevails.

The three-year master's degree plan is not simply a theoretical outline. In its main features it is already in operation in twenty-eight institutions as an experimental program. It has been discussed with graduate and undergraduate deans and with university presidents and faculty members. Many see in it the possible answer to a number of basic problems, such as the identification of talent, the early recognition of that talent in the program of study prescribed, a chance for improvement of the articulation of graduate and undergraduate education, a device for recruiting Ph.D. candidates, a means of shortening the time lag between the B.A. and the Ph.D., and, finally, an opportunity to develop interest in and morale for college teaching as a profession, through faculty advisers and a program planned by the faculty and upper-class college and graduate students.

In advanced work beyond the master's degree, it is proposed that there be two Doctor of Philosophy degrees, designated as Ph.D. and D.Phil. The former would be used as the title for the advanced degree for scientific, technological, and professional students not planning to enter college teaching. The D.Phil. would be designed especially for college and university teaching in the basic arts and science subjects. A dissertation would be required for this degree as well as for the Ph.D., though in the natural sciences a somewhat greater specialization in research would be expected of the Ph.D. than of the D.Phil. student. On the other hand, one or two basic courses, such as the "Role of Science in the Modern World" or the "Philosophy of University Education," might be a requirement for the D.Phil.

The gateway to the D.Phil. would usually be the three-year master's degree. The normal time for the D.Phil. in such cases would be two years beyond the master's. All capable master's candidates under this plan should be encouraged in every way to continue on to the doctorate. Further details of this program will be found in the chapter that outlines the Doctor of Philosophy degree.

In addition, this report contains some discussion of the needs for post-doctoral work. The demand for work beyond the doctor's degree is essentially a development of the mid-century decade. Before 1950 there were so few post-doctoral students that they did not constitute a problem for the university administrators, but by 1960, in the stronger universities, it was beginning to loom large. Post-doctoral fellowships have been partly responsible for this development, but the need for more research training than can be provided through the doctor's dissertation is chiefly responsible. All indications point to a growing need in this area and to the necessity for taking this into account in future university planning.

The program outlined in Part 2 will include suggestions for meeting this new and expanding demand on graduate education. In the final chapter two considerations are paramount: (1) such changes in curriculum and procedures as will enable the graduate school to meet current demands more adequately, and (2) such new developments and plans as will be required to meet future needs. It is important that the demands upon graduate education ten and twenty years from now, so far as we are able to envision them, should be given consideration. Unless sound organization and planning in graduate education are begun early, there is little chance that the universities will be able to meet their responsibility in 1970 or 1980.

CHAPTER 1

The Strategic Role of Graduate Education

No segment of higher education has so significant a role to play as the graduate school during the seventh decade of this century. It is the pace setter for the enterprise. Much depends upon its effectiveness during this critical period, when college and university enrollments will be climbing to an unprecedented high. This vast horde will require more instruction, more guidance, and more wise leadership than any previous generation of students. Despite statements to the contrary, a crisis has developed which can be met only by a revitalized graduate education program.

College teaching is the most critical area, but provision for other professions, all of which are expanding, is also a crucial need, and it is the university graduate school that has the responsibility for setting the tone of professional as well as undergraduate teaching. Medicine, law, science, engineering, nursing, business administration, and a host of other professions are increasingly requiring *graduate* work—the *graduate doctor's* degree for the teacher in the professional school. Many professional schools give their own graduate degrees, but this is unfortunate. Some of the stronger universities have successfully resisted this pressure, and a vigorous, well-organized, and effective graduate program will in time, it is hoped, bring back under the umbrella of one university-wide graduate college all phases of advanced work.

While the teaching profession needs now twice as many Ph.D.

12

holders as are being produced, the pressure from government, business, and industry is no less severe. The more than four thousand industrial laboratories in the country and the vast research programs conducted by the government must have more and more men and women with maximum training, not only in science and technology but in economics, management, psychology, and other fields. As an example of the growth in industrial research activities, it will suffice to cite the figures given in the preface to the tenth edition of *Industrial Research Laboratories of the United States*:[1] the first edition, in 1921, listed 290 companies; the tenth, in 1956, listed 4,060 companies, operating 4,834 laboratories.

The graduate schools are grappling with a triple-headed monster—the research needs of the country: for teachers, for pure scientists, and for an almost limitless number of applied scientists in business, industry, and government. It is a far cry from the day when the department of advanced studies or the graduate schools were held responsible for a handful of students who wanted to proceed beyond the first degree. Only within the last half-century has graduate education become a major division of the university.

Next to the junior college, the graduate school is the youngest of the organized segments of higher education. The first American university to adopt the German idea of research and to add it to the college, which was derived from the British, was Johns Hopkins. This practice spread slowly. With the exception of a few of the best endowed and most advanced universities, graduate and research programs were limited. It was not until after World War I that the conception of the modern university began to shape the course of things to come in university education. In 1926 the number of graduate students was less than one fifth of the number in 1958, and the number of earned doctorates in 1926 was less than one sixth of the number in 1958. In short, it was less than fifty years ago that graduate education

[1] *Industrial Research Laboratories of the United States* (10th ed.; Washington, D. C.: National Research Council, 1956), p. 1.

became a problem of any magnitude from the standpoint of the numbers of students or of the demands for its products.

The explosion of interest in graduate education occurred after 1945. The dramatic demonstration of the magic of scientific research was the discovery of atomic fission. Government funds financed it, but it was university scientists who actually performed what to most people was a modern miracle. It suggested also to industry the possibilities of research if adequately supported. Thus, from being a minor enterprise before World War II, research in the last decade has become one of the major industries of the country. It has developed so rapidly that it has caught the graduate schools off guard.

This accounts for the fact that the largest single unfilled need in the American economy is for more and better scientists, more and better researchers, and more adequate support for educating them. Not only do economic and educational needs require it, but it is recognized as essential to long-range defense as well. Top future leadership in all phases of American life— economic, scientific, political, and industrial—will require more than the first degree. Those who aspire to positions of influence and constructive leadership will move into graduate schools that are prepared to receive them and to give them the proper instruction. This means that the graduate schools are on the brink of the largest expansion in their history.

In planning for the future of higher education, the emphasis has been on the expansion of undergraduate enrollments and the ways of meeting their needs, whereas the most critical area from every standpoint is the graduate school. Much has been said about the shortage of teachers and the need for larger output of Ph.D. graduates, but relatively little concrete and constructive planning has been done to meet the graduate school needs. The passage of the National Defense Education Act indicates a recognition, on the part of the Federal Government, of the needs for graduate students, and the Woodrow Wilson Fund contributed by the philanthropic foundations is evidence that private agencies are ready to assist, but the planning on the part of the educators for a new and revitalized educational program has been disappointing.

In some quarters it is argued that the need for college and university teachers is grossly exaggerated. To begin with, attention is called to the fact that the President's Committee on Education beyond the High School erred in suggesting that three hundred thousand "teaching faculty" would be needed by 1960. As proof, the fact is cited that there were only two hundred thousand in 1958.[2] Its validity is based on the assumption that colleges and universities were adequately staffed in that year. All reports of studies indicate that by 1958 the faculty-student ratio had decreased, and particularly the ratio of adequately trained staff to total faculty had dropped markedly.

Beginning with an essentially false assumption, the author of *Graduate Education in the United States*[3] projects estimates of needs based upon the ratios of 1 teacher to 14, to 16, to 18, to 20 students, and concludes that there is no crisis, only a problem. Certain basic facts are ignored. First, relatively few institutions of quality have as low a ratio as 1 teaching staff member to 18 or even to 16 students; while the small prestige colleges and universities have more than 1 to 14 students, and these are the institutions that can attract the Ph.D. graduates. Many institutions consider a ratio of 1 to 8, 10, or 12 students to be normal. By juggling the ratio of teachers to students, one can come out with any figure that is desired, but it is an unrealistic one.

Everyone is aware of the fact that the percentage of Ph.D.'s on college and university staffs has dropped sharply since 1950 and is continuing to drop, when what is sorely needed is a sharp rise in the preparation of teachers with maximum training, in view of the significant issues that face the United States in the nineteen-sixties. The ratio of 1 teacher to 18 or 20 students may be "grass roots arithmetic," but it is not a true statistic. In view of the amount of research expected of university professors

[2] Bernard Berelson, *Graduate Education in the United States* (New York: McGraw-Hill Book Co., Inc., 1960), p. 70.
[3] *Ibid.*, p. 78.

and of the increase in the number of graduate students, the ratio of teachers to students should be rising just to maintain the quality of instructional services, and no one should be willing to settle for the status quo with respect to quality. We must not only care for greater numbers of students but also improve the quality of instruction. On the matter of *quality* there is consensus among not only educators but also the lay public.

As we shall see later, the number of doctorates is not a true index of the number of degree holders qualified for classroom teaching. While the report for 1958 showed that only four thousand of the nine thousand Ph.D. graduates took positions in business, industry, and government, leaving five thousand to enter educational work, it is not recognized that many who pursue an educational career do not become college teachers. For example, 18 per cent of all doctorates in 1958 were in professional education, and many of these went into administrative positions in the public schools. Likewise, in agriculture many of the doctorates go into experiment stations which are part of the land-grant college program but do not involve teaching. Also, doctorates in such subjects as anatomy, bacteriology, biochemistry, entomology, et cetera, go into research mainly in medical centers.

These facts have not been sufficiently taken into account in reckoning the number available for college teaching positions. Furthermore, much of the increase in the number of doctorates produced in recent years has come from agricultural, engineering, or medical science divisions. In most previous studies this fact has not been brought out; yet it is an important consideration in our efforts to determine the need for an increased supply of doctorates.

For example, in the twelve-year period from 1926 to 1937 the average annual production of doctorates in all areas of engineering, including aeronautical, mechanical, civil, electrical, chemical, and others, was 46.5, whereas in 1958 the figure was 646.[4]

[4] *American Universities and Colleges* (8th ed.; American Council on Education, 1960), p. 1146.

Presumably most of these Ph.D.'s enter shools of engineering, *๛* but until recently these schools did not ordinarily require doctorates of teachers. This is but another way of saying that the same percentage of doctorates on university faculties will not go as far as it did fifteen to twenty years ago, because new subject fields in the university complex are requiring doctorates for their teaching staff. Other fields than engineering are also developing in the same direction, with the result that the proportion of doctorates left to man regular college classrooms is dropping rapidly.

Somewhat related to these considerations are the growing demands of the junior or community colleges, which began at the turn of the century and now enroll twice as many students as the graduate schools. It is reported that about 10 per cent of the faculties of these institutions hold the doctor's degree. The implication in a recent study was that this is sufficient and that as the enrollments in these institutions increase, the number of Ph.D.'s required to staff higher education will tend to be smaller. The fact is that the reason the two-year institutions have so few teachers with maximum training is that they are not available. High schools are more and more requiring the master's degree of their teachers. It is only a question of time before all secondary school teachers will be required to have the first graduate degree before securing a permanent appointment. In the light of this fact, junior and community colleges will doubtless require at least 25 per cent of their staffs to have the doctorate as soon as possible; this is desirable since more than one half of the graduates of these institutions now transfer to advanced work. A move to increase from 10 to 25 per cent the number of Ph.D.'s in these institutions would greatly increase the demand for doctorates. Thus, the expansion of the two-year colleges will increase, rather than diminish, the pressure on the graduate schools.

In any realistic consideration of and planning for the demands for graduate work, a number of factors must be recognized and accounted for. First, there is the growing demand of the public for better-trained personnel. At the beginning of this century a graduate of a two-year normal school was deemed well qualified to teach in an elementary school. Indeed, a vast number of the teachers then employed had much less than that—a first-, second-, or third-grade certificate which was secured by examination. The certificate examinations have passed; the two-year normal school no longer exists. A four-year college course is now considered the minimum qualification for teaching in the modern elementary school. Most normal schools of fifty years ago are now state colleges or universities which give not only the bachelor's but the master's degree. Some now grant the Doctor of Education degree. All along the line the trend is upward.

The Ph.D. degree until recently was considered the termination of formal university education. It is still the highest degree awarded, but in many of the stronger universities the demand for post-doctorate training is so great as to pose a serious problem. Post-doctoral fellowships are now common in major universities, and the demand for work beyond the Ph.D. is in its infancy. Within another decade this will expand until special provision will have to be made by universities to meet it. It will devolve upon the graduate schools to plan these provisions, perhaps in collaboration with the professional schools.

In every area the demand for more and better training characterizes American society. Doctors and lawyers, formerly apprenticed to a practitioner for a year or two, could take examinations and thus be admitted to the profession. Now a college degree is usually essential for admission to the professional school. Then three to four years of intensive training are required before admission to the state examination is permitted. In addition, in medicine three to five years of internships and residencies are required before one is admitted to specialty board examinations which qualify one as a surgeon, an internist, a gynecologist, or a pediatrician.

It is not inconceivable that before the end of this century the program of advanced studies in the universities in all areas will follow the lead of medicine. The Ph.D. degree may be followed by two, three, or more years of post-doctoral work as preparation for posts requiring a high degree of specialization. It is in that perspective that the future need for graduate education should be considered. Graduate faculties and councils will naturally be looked to for leadership in this development. The imaginative and creative abilities that they have exhibited as scientists and scholars will need to be focused on the long-range needs and developments that the future will surely require.

But the expansion upward is not the only problem that will need to be reviewed, studied, and solved by universities through their graduate faculties. A situation that has troubled thoughtful educators for some years results from the demands of industry and government on universities for types of research that should be performed by other agencies. In other English-speaking countries there are independent agencies supported by industry which conduct researches that the universities here are called on to perform. In Britain this agency is the Department of Scientific and Industrial Research (D.S.I.R.); in India and South Africa, the Council for Scientific and Industrial Research (C.S.I.R.). Other Commonwealth countries have similar agencies. In addition, Britain now has ten colleges of advanced technology which train technologists and conduct researches for business and industry. In Europe such activities are carried on by research institutes.

In the United States the Mellon Institute, the Southern Research Institute, the Stanford Research Institute, and the Southwest Research Institute perform much the same function as the departments and councils referred to above. In addition, the larger industries and some of the smaller ones have laboratories of their own, through which many of their research needs are met.

Despite the work of the institutes and the independent and industrial laboratories, so great is the need for research that the universities are called on to help out. Someone has suggested that the direction of university research is determined no longer by the universities but by outside pressures. The government actually provides most of the funds that support their research activities, but business and industry also seek help from these institutions. More than half of the budgets of some universities are for research, support for which is provided by outside agencies.

Unquestionably the situation should be examined with care, and some policy should be developed to insure the integrity of the universities as institutions of higher learning rather than as research stations for governmental, industrial, and commercial agencies. Initiative in such a review and study would seem to be the responsibility of the graduate schools, but as yet there is no organization that can speak for graduate education as a whole. Studies can and should be made on each campus, but these obviously could not establish a national policy that might serve as a guide for all institutions engaging in contract research.

A varied assortment of other problems—such as recruitment, articulation of graduate and undergraduate work, preparation of college teachers, and the whole gamut of graduate school methods, procedures, and results—awaits consideration and action by the graduate school. They are cited here to indicate the vastness of the opportunity and the responsibility of this strategic segment of higher education. To meet the responsibilities and to exploit the opportunities are tasks too great to be entrusted to a part-time faculty presided over by a dean who has no authority.

With all the shortcomings of its organization and of its procedures, the graduate school has achieved a unique place among the schools of the universities. Its graduates, the Ph.D. holders, occupy a position of prestige that cannot be matched by those of other divisions. Whether they command that respect because they are relatively so rare, because they have taken so long to win the coveted prize, or because on the whole their achievements have been so outstanding, it would be difficult to say. Perhaps all three factors have contributed to their prestige. Hence, with all the criticisms of these divisions of our universities which will appear in subsequent chapters, the author is not unaware of their virtues as well.

Not only higher education but the whole American economy owes a great debt to the graduate schools and their products, for they have made America research-conscious, and, thus, indirectly have been responsible for the great economic and industrial progress of the past century. Science, which began to attract attention before the middle of the nineteenth century, established laboratories for research, and technology, which followed shortly afterward, added to these facilities. They marked a turning point in university education, for they introduced the empirical method and the pioneering spirit into scholarship. Scientists and technologists emphasized early the search for knowledge. They became the real pioneers in the new type of higher learning, which is bent upon pushing back the frontiers of knowledge. This is the motivation of modern research and graduate work.

There were, of course, many research scholars, working in their ivory towers, before the advent of science and technology, but their efforts were not recognized by the university as a part of its function. There were no graduate schools until after science and technology had become integral parts of universities, for it was only then that research was recognized as an essential university activity.

Harvard established a graduate school in 1872; John Hopkins, founded in 1876, with a major emphasis upon research from the beginning, and Chicago, opening in 1891 (the first institution to announce, through its president, that among its purposes teaching was secondary to research), were among the pioneers. Departments of advanced studies, and the graduate schools that developed from them in these and other universities, have carried the torch for this new activity of the university and of higher learning. Though less than one hundred years old as an organized university activity, graduate education and research have in that period probably influenced the life of society more than any other one division of the university, because they have stimulated the professional schools, government, business, and industry to emphasize research as a means of progress. The spirit of inquiry, investigation, and discovery, which was responsible for the new industrial revolution of the mid-nineteenth century, antedated the development of graduate and research work, but the crystallization of this spirit into an institution, the graduate school, consciously devoted to fostering research as one of its chief purposes, was the contribution that higher education made to this revolutionary movement. Institutionalizing the concept of "progress through discovery" by universities is responsible for a new industry—research—which is now a sixteen-billion-dollar enterprise. The Federal Government alone is spending nine billion dollars this year for research.

These comments on the significance of graduate education and research are made with the hope of providing a perspective, a framework within which to assess their future role. The achievements of the past for which advanced studies and research have been responsible are but a token of what may be expected in the future. There is little doubt that graduate education, which now accounts for less than 10 per cent of the college and university population, will reach 20 to 25 per cent before the end of the century. This prediction is based upon the theory that many able students who, for one reason or another, are now lost to higher education in high school and college will be identified, encouraged, and held in the program, and that a higher degree of selection will be exercised in the future than in the past.

With this belief in the future of graduate education, one must view with some concern the present weaknesses in the program, methods, and procedures. Are graduate schools, as organized and conducted, able to meet the demands of the future? In 1959-1960 the graduate school population reached 305,000. What will it be in 1975 or 1985? It rose from less than 10,000 in 1910 to more than 300,000 in 1960. The over-all college and university population in that period increased less than tenfold, while the number of graduate students increased more than thirtyfold.

With the growth of graduate schools the problems will multiply. There will be a demand for putting graduate students on a rigorous and regular program like medical or law students: those who drop out will risk not being able to return, because others will take their places. Such a program should produce not only more scholars and scientists but better ones. The post-doctoral demands may mount faster than the pre-doctoral ones, and to meet them graduate school procedures may have to be streamlined. It may be possible to do this without lowering standards.

In addition to internal problems, matters of national policy with respect to sponsored research, to allowance for overhead costs in contracts, to the extent to which a university faculty is justified in spending its time on either government or industrial projects, to the relation of graduate students to research done under contract, should be explored. In these and other national policy matters an organization representing all universities offering the Ph.D. degree should be much more effective than any agency that now exists.

Other problems more basic than any of those mentioned so far relate to the whole structure of higher education. Mr. McGrath suggests that the graduate school is responsible for the decline of the liberal arts. If that be true, it has been engaged in undermining its own foundations, for all will agree that a strong liberal arts college training is essential to preparation for graduate work. Mr. McGrath has had a long and distinguished career as college teacher, college dean, university president, and United States Commissioner of Education. He has long been a thoughtful student of American education. Without arguing the merits of his contention, when such a conclusion is reached by one with his long experience and study of our system, it cannot be ignored or considered lightly. It suggests the need for rethinking the relation of the college to the graduate and professional schools. The professional schools have a stake in the college, too, for they depend upon it to provide the basic education needed by all professional students. Such a study, to be effective, would require representatives of the college and of the graduate and professional schools.

Discontent has been expressed by educational leaders about the nature of the dissertation and the intensive specialization the Ph.D. requires. These considerations, and many others, are always raised when college teacher preparation is discussed. There have also been complaints about the types of dissertation subject that are found particularly in the humanistic-social studies fields. Too detailed and trivial in scope, in purpose, in the type of mental discipline required; too much emphasis on facts and too little on ideas and concepts; uninspiring in subject matter; and unworthy of the research required for the highest academic award, the Ph.D. degree—are some of the objections. A few examples will illustrate: "A Comparison of the Forethoughts of Sixth-Grade Students Concerning the First Year of Junior High School with Reality as seen through their Afterthoughts at the end of the First Year of Junior High School," "Some Correlates of Social Awareness," "An Experimental Study of Relative Deprivation and Relative Reward," "An Investigation of the Listening Proficiency of Stutterers," "An Evaluation of the Dale Carnegie Course and similar programs at Brooklyn College," "Economic Decision-Making in Hog Feeding—A New Approach," and "Distribution of Empty Freight Cars."[5]

Perhaps dissertations on these subjects have some use, but are they appropriate topics for research on the basis of which the Ph.D. degree is granted? Do they represent American *higher learning?* Are there no basic issues in the social science areas that could provide more suitable topics for study and investigation? What does research on such subjects mean as a contribution to knowledge, as a means of educating the students who engage in it, or as a test of their intellectual abilities? One seeks in vain for a satisfactory philosophy of graduate education into which such topics will fit.

We are living in an age when ideological conflict is characteristic. Totalitarianism, nazism, fascism, communism, socialism,

[5] *Dissertation Abstracts* (Ann Arbor, Mich.: University Microfilms, Inc., 1960), XXI, No. 1.

and democracy have been debated constantly for fifty years. Two world wars, the Korean conflict, the founding of the United Nations, a revolution in transportation, in medicine (through discovery and use of antibiotics), and in race relations —all these and many other social, economic, and political changes have occurred in this century, yet dissertation abstracts give little hint that anything important has been taking place. If our most capable young scholars ignore what is happening in the world about them and find nothing more significant to engage their research efforts than subjects such as those listed above, what is the hope for the future?

These young people are not responsible for the situation. The educational system is at fault. More specifically, it is largely the fault of the leaders in *graduate education*. If the colleges have failed to stimulate an interest in the great issues of our time, it is still largely the responsibility of the graduate schools, whose products constitute the college teaching personnel. Surely the time has come for educational leadership to forsake the narrow specialization on essentially trivial subjects and to begin to direct the research efforts of youth toward basic ideas, general concepts, and issues that have relevance in the modern world. If it entails revolutionary reforms in graduate education, that will not be impossible if the present leadership is convinced of the need.

What is said of the social sciences applies equally to the humanities. There was never a time in the history of Western civilization when its basic tenets have been under more severe attack than in this century. We have fought two world wars to preserve them and, since the last one, have been engaged in a running battle with an opposing ideology. Despite this situation, the dissertation abstracts from our universities reflect little or nothing of the great historic struggles of our time. The number of young scholars seeking Ph.D.'s in these fields has declined in proportion to those engaged in scientific and technological research. The availability of scholarship and fellowship funds in science and technology may be largely responsible for more graduate students in these fields, but the unresolved type of research in the humanities and the social sciences may also have contributed to the result.

The public's concern that we maintain superiority in science and technology, and the fear that we might lose it, have led to the emphasis upon pure and applied science since World War II. The basis for this attitude is substantial: our national defense is involved. Though we must, at least temporarily, give scientific and technological research and development high priority, it must not blind us to the fact that long-range needs suggest that intelligent faith in our humanistic and social heritage is also a basic element in national defense and integrity.

Unfortunately our educational programs fail to take adequate account of this fact. Neither the college nor the graduate school has adjusted its program to a systematic consideration of the great ideas and ideals that constitute the foundations of Western culture. What a gold mine of material for master's theses and Ph.D. dissertations is to be found in the excavation of the ideas that underlie the concepts of democracy, of inalienable rights, of the dignity of the individual, of justice, of freedom in all its forms, of the rights incorporated in our Bill of Rights, and many others that are the motivations of a free society. A tracing of these concepts in the history, literature, and philosophy of our culture should provide the core of the liberal arts college and a sound approach for graduate study in the field of the humanities.

The national interest in other lands, in international relations, and in the understanding of other cultures since World War II has resulted in a growing recognition of the importance of these areas in the curriculum. In tracing the ideals and concepts upon which our way of life rests, the student would be led to other cultures where they had originated and developed. Thus, the student would acquire a knowledge and an appreciation of other peoples that are not possible through the usual arts courses, and would as a result develop greater interest in what is happening in the rest of the world.

The new concern for what goes on elsewhere, which has developed as a result of modern means of transportation and of our relations with so many underdeveloped countries, provides a fertile soil for the cultivation of more vital humanistic-social studies. The colleges and universities have been slow in exploiting these possibilities. The events of recent decades have profoundly affected work in the natural sciences. They should have had a similar effect on the humanities and social sciences, but to date they have not. This reform is bound to occur if we are to have a revitalized humanistic-social studies curriculum and a well-rounded educational program.

The reforms suggested for the college as well as for the graduate school can take place only if the graduate education leaders take the initiative and provide the kind of education needed by those who will teach in the college. Thus, the role of the graduate school, in effecting fundamental changes in higher education, is unique. No other agency can take its place. The responsibility of this segment of the university is therefore enormous.

CHAPTER 2

Graduate Education in the Changing Scene

During the twenty years between the First and Second World Wars great ferment and change occurred in all areas of the university program. In the arts college, survey, interdepartmental, and honors courses were developed. Each flourished for a time and then ceased to attract attention. The dissatisfaction with the curriculum, with the proliferation of courses, with the superficiality and lack of purpose in the program as a whole, gave rise also to the general education movement.

In the professional schools deep discontent prevailed, and widespread efforts at reform were undertaken. It was in this period that modern medicine came of age. The "B" Class medical schools were eliminated by 1928, and the support for the "A" Class schools that survived was multiplied manyfold. Various studies which led to reforms in the areas of legal, engineering, nursing, and dental education are recorded in that period. While World War II retarded the march of progress, when it was over there were renewed efforts on the part of the colleges and professional schools to strengthen their programs.

The general education movement at Harvard, Yale, Brown, Columbia, Chicago, and other colleges was evidence of the ferment on the undergraduate level after World War II. The efforts to improve undergraduate education were not confined to the ranking universities. Hundreds of institutions throughout the country engaged in studies of the curriculum, in experimentation, in a variety of efforts to give new vitality to the college program.

Schools of medicine in some instances added social scientists to the faculty. Drastic reforms in medical education were instituted at Western Reserve University, while more modest efforts were in evidence in many other medical schools.

Legal education was included in a five-year study of the legal profession, which its leaders conducted with the aid of substantial foundation support. While no major changes were effected as a result of that study, many improvements in curriculum and methods were noted in various sections of the country.

Studies of nursing and of architectural and theological education resulted in many changes in these areas. The teachers colleges and university schools of education experienced even more significant changes. Greater liberal arts content characterized the new curriculum, and there were more effective professional courses. Many state teachers colleges became state colleges, or universities in some instances, indicating a change in emphasis.

In 1957 when Sputnik appeared, the Western world was shocked. In the United States a clamor arose about the ineffectiveness of our scientific and technological education. It had been assumed that the United States and Britain were in the vanguard of scientific and technological development, until the Russian exhibit made it clear to the world that, at least in one area, Russia had achieved superiority.

The criticism of American education since that time has been widespread and bitter. New emphasis upon science and technology, a new concern for quality and excellence, larger sums for finding talent and seeing that it is developed, and greater public awareness of the fundamental importance of scientific progress have been the outcome. The Federal Government has made grants to strengthen graduate education, to attract more talented youth into the profession of teaching, to strengthen foreign language study, to provide loans for housing in order to accommodate an increasing number of college and university students, etc.

At no period in the history of the American Republic has there been such an intense interest on the part of the public in education at all levels as there is now. By the same token, there are perhaps greater dissatisfaction, more concern, and less confidence in the achievements of the educational system than there were previously. The criticism of the public, the discontent of the educators, and the growing interest of government, business, and industry in improving the program, particularly at the higher levels, are elements in the picture of the post-war period.

The division of the university that has been relatively unaffected by what has occurred since 1920 is the graduate school. Despite the studies, symposiums, and criticisms of its program, it has undergone no basic changes in curriculum, method, or procedures since World War I—indeed, since 1900. In contrast with efforts of the leaders in undergraduate and professional education to modify and strengthen their programs, the leaders in graduate education have appeared content with the status quo. Any suggestion of basic change in organization or procedure is promptly rejected. The question arises whether this is justified. Let us examine the record.

In his study at Columbia,[1] Rosenhaupt pointed out that of the 4,725 students who began graduate work at Columbia between 1940 and 1956, 2,869 had received no degree at all by 1958. Only 1,705 had been awarded the master's degree, and 151 the doctorate. This means that out of an enrollment of nearly 5,000 graduate students, only 39 per cent received any degree, and only 3.2 per cent received the doctorate. Such waste of time and energy on the part of both students and faculty can mean only one of two things, or perhaps both: the students were poorly selected or were mistreated by the graduate faculties. Since it is the faculties who set admission standards, they must accept responsibility for the outcome whatever the cause.

[1] Hans Rosenhaupt, *Graduate Students Experience at Columbia University, 1940-1956* (New York: Columbia University Press, 1958), pp. 84-5.

What happened to those who were lucky enough to earn the coveted Ph.D.? How long did it take them to achieve their goal? From Table 56[2] in the Rosenhaupt study we have extracted a few subject fields that are usually taught in college. The average time spent in pursuit of the Ph.D. in these subjects, after admission to graduate school, was as follows:

English	10.1	years
History	9.5	"
Mathematics	7.4	"
Physics	7.0	"
German	12.5	"
French	9.7	"
Greek & Latin	10.9	"
Chemistry	5.3	"
Psychology	5.5	"
Sociology	10.1	"

Mr. Rosenhaupt called attention to the decline in the percentage of Ph.D.'s on college and university faculties, pointing out that whereas in 1957 it was 40, by 1970 it would probably be only 20. Developments since 1957 indicate that this estimate was conservative: unless some drastic revision of methods and procedures is effected in graduate schools, it may be even less than 20 per cent. In the light of these facts, if the attitude of the graduate schools is one of complacency, it is not simply critical but alarming.

The question whether the experience at Columbia is typical, may arise. Certainly Harvard, Yale, and Princeton have better records. But Princeton, which has the best of the three, graduates with the Ph.D. only 60 per cent of those who have passed the qualifying examinations. Throughout the country the lag between the B.A. and the Ph.D. is a matter of deep concern in view of the shortage of college teachers with maximum training.

The Southern Regional Education Board made a recent

2 *Ibid.*, p. 124.

TABLE 1

AVERAGE B.A.-PH.D. TIME LAPSE IN VARIOUS DOCTORATE
FIELDS FOR CERTAIN INSTITUTIONAL CLASSIFICATIONS
1950-1956

	Institutions Producing fewer than 50 doctorates Prior to 1950		Institutions Producing more than 50 doctorates Prior to 1950		All Institutions	
	(N-13)		(N-25)			
Field	Degrees 1950-56	Mean Time Lapse (Years)	Degrees 1950-56	Mean Time Lapse (Years)	Degrees 1950-56	Mean Time Lapse (Years)
Physical Sciences	1532	8.0	637	7.8	2169	7.9
Mathematics	178	10.5	69	8.8	247	10.0
Physics & Astronomy	393	7.8	40	10.8	433	8.1
Chemistry	688	7.1	358	6.9	1046	7.0
Earth Sciences	76	8.7	*	*	81	8.6
Engineering	197	9.0	165	8.6	362	8.8
Biological Sciences	810	8.4	380	9.3	1190	8.7
Agriculture	12	8.2	22	8.8	34	8.6
Botany	118	8.7	26	8.1	144	8.6
Biochemistry	64	7.9	35	7.8	99	7.9
Genetics	*	*	17	10.2	20	9.4
Microbiology	104	8.1	21	9.9	125	8.4
Physiology	52	7.0	38	7.7	90	7.3
Zoology	173	8.5	61	9.8	234	8.8
Biosciences, Miscellaneous	193	8.5	156	9.9	349	9.1
Medical Sciences	91	9.0	*	*	95	9.1
Social Sciences	1064	9.8	208	9.1	1272	9.7
Sociology	113	11.1	10	11.8	123	11.1
Economics	171	10.5	33	10.0	204	10.5
Geography	32	10.5	*	*	34	11.1
History	295	11.4	41	10.7	336	11.3
Political Science	108	9.8	*	*	109	9.8
Psychology	345	7.6	121	7.9	466	7.7
Education	732	14.9	301	15.8	1033	15.2
Arts and Humanities	668	12.3	92	13.0	760	12.3
Business	54	12.6	*	*	63	11.9
Foreign Languages & Literature	145	11.6	20	15.3	165	12.1
Arts and Music	14	13.6	11	13.7	25	13.6
English Language & Literature						
Philosophy	37	7.4			37	7.4
Religion	46	11.0			46	11.0
Speech	38	15.4	*	*	44	14.3
Other	13	9.9	10	12.4	23	11.0

* Averages not computed where fewer than ten degrees were conferred.

TABLE 2

Number of Doctorates and Average B.A.-Ph.D. Time Lapse for the Period 1950-1956 by Five Major Doctorate Areas

Twenty Selected Southern Institutions

Institutions*	Physical Sciences Degrees	Mean	Biological Sciences Degrees	Mean	Social Sciences Degrees	Mean	Education Degrees	Mean	Arts & Humanities Degrees	Mean
University of Texas	321	8.2	101	8.0	228	10.2	180	15.8	138	14.0
Johns Hopkins	249	8.2	134	9.1	83	8.1	10	16.1	85	8.5
North Carolina University	145	8.9	59	8.1	188	10.7	59	14.6	129	12.1
Duke	126	6.8	98	8.0	128	9.8	17	15.0	82	11.3
University of Maryland	120	9.0	174	8.2	61	9.1	64	15.0	18	15.5
University of Virginia	116	6.6	20	10.7	76	9.4	23	15.6	31	12.5
Louisiana State University	71	7.4	68	8.7	49	10.9	35	13.8	54	12.6
University of Florida	118	9.1	84	8.0	47	9.9	93	13.6	35	10.2
George Peabody	**		**		23	10.4	133	14.2	17	17.1
Vanderbilt	67	7.3	27	8.0	54	8.6	**		47	12.4
University of Oklahoma	67	8.5	25	8.6	37	8.5	73	15.9	11	13.8
University of Kentucky	42	7.2	**		86	10.1	45	15.0	17	15.4
University of Tennessee	98	8.6	42	7.4	48	7.6	53	14.6	10	14.1
Tulane	53	6.8	35	9.0	32	8.0	**		29	13.3
Texas A & M	48	9.7	91	10.5	**		**		**	
Rice Institute	81	5.8	16	7.0	**		**		**	
Oklahoma A & M	40	8.0	55	9.8	**		46	17.9	**	
North Carolina State	35	9.2	76	7.8	23	9.7	**		**	
University of Delaware	136	6.0	**		**		**		**	
Florida State University	28	6.8	**		23	8.6	28	16.0	26	12.0

* Listed in order of total doctorate production 1936-1956.
** Not computed when fewer than ten degrees were granted in the area.

study of the situation in fourteen Southern states. The results are indicated in tables one and two.

It is clear from this study that Columbia's experience is not atypical. The picture in all sections of the country is largely the same. The degree that is publicized as requiring three years of study beyond the bachelor of arts turns out in actual practice to require, on the average, seven to twelve years.

The increase in the number of doctorates awarded each year is cited in support of the view that all is *well* or reasonably *well* with graduate education. For example, in the twelve-year period from 1926 to 1937 the average number of doctorates awarded annually was 2,156, in the ten year period from 1938 to 1947 the average was 2,538, while in 1958 it was 8,942. Should not one be reassured when confronted with these facts? The number of doctorates has increased some fourfold, while the undergraduate student body has increased only threefold in round figures. The answer is found in an analysis of the type of doctorate and the fields in which it was awarded.

In 1958 the number of doctorates awarded in ten fields, as compared with averages in other years, will illustrate:[3]

TABLE 3

Subject	1958	Average per year 1938-1947	Average per year 1926-1937			
Agriculture	309	59.4	46.2 — 6.4	fold	increase	
Chemistry	939	434.8	375 — 2.5	"	"	
Education	2,425	293	267 — 9.0	"	"	
Psychology	727	97.4	90 — 8.0	"	"	
Theology	252	78.1	50.1 — 5	"	"	
English	333	146	124.3 — 2.6	"	"	
Mathematics	247	68	67.7 — 3.6	"	"	
History	297	122	120.8 — 2.4	"	"	
Physics	464	116	110.6 — 4.2	"	"	
Economics	310	118	117.5 — 2.6	"	"	

Not only have non-college subject fields been increasing more rapidly than the standard subjects in the production of doctorates, as represented by the ten areas cited above, but new

[3] *American Universities and Colleges* (8th ed.; American Council on Education, 1960), p. 1146.

areas have developed doctoral programs, and other fields have increased their production of doctorates enormously. For example, anatomy, bacteriology, biochemistry, entomology, forestry, pharmacy, physiology, public health, veterinary medicine, and other biological sciences not studied in college account for a total of 1,297 of the 8,942 doctorates listed for 1958. If to these we add engineering, theology, education, agriculture, and chemistry which are at least mainly professional (judged by the number entering teaching), the impressive total of 5,869 of the doctorates produced in 1958 did not prepare the recipients for teaching in colleges. This leaves only 3,073 available to man the college classrooms and laboratories. A few from chemistry did enter teaching, but they were more than offset by the number of psychology doctorates that failed to enter teaching.

From this analysis it is clear that the number of doctorates awarded each year is not a true index of the number available for college teaching. Many of the Ph.D.'s enter teaching in agricultural, medical, engineering education, and theological schools and, hence, are counted among the 5,000 that enter the profession, but they do not represent a source of supply for the colleges where the need is greatest. Since the quality of college preparation affects all the professions for which they prepare, a decline of standards in this segment of higher education is a threat not only to the professions but to the quality of American culture itself.

In the light of these facts, the status of graduate education in the United States appears to represent a major crisis rather than a simple problem. How has this situation been allowed to develop when for more than twenty years leaders in American education have urged reforms? Fred Keppel, in his 1938 annual report to the Carnegie Corporation, and Walter Jessup, in his 1944 report to the Carnegie Foundation, were among those who called attention to the lethargy of the graduate schools and the need for change. Many have wondered why, when reforms were taking place in the colleges and the professional schools, no significant changes have occurred in the graduate schools.

The changes occurring in the undergraduate program, in the various professional areas, and in science and technology, while the graduate schools have remained unchanged, have produced a strange lack of articulation between undergraduate and professional education on the one hand and graduate education on the other. Though the majority of those who complete graduate work may enter the teaching profession, the graduate schools in the main have taken no account of the changes in the colleges and in the professional schools. Their graduates, generally speaking, have had the same kind of education as their predecessors of fifty years ago. Perhaps some would argue that the goal of work beyond the college should be "scholarship," a zeal for learning, for pioneering, in an effort to push back the frontiers of knowledge, on the ground that these are the qualities most needed in the teachers of youth. This argument might have some validity if every college graduate expected to become a specialist in some field of scholarship. Since this is obviously not the case, other facts must be taken into account.

Surely the goals of the college that have emerged since 1920, and the new methods employed to achieve them, must not be overlooked by those who plan the education of future college teachers. To ignore them would be comparable to the medical schools' ignoring the advances in medicine since 1920 in the education of future doctors. If the retort be that the graduate school is not a professional school and should not be compared with one, the answer is simple. It is the only agency engaged in the education of college and university teachers, and a substantial proportion of its products enter that profession. It cannot, therefore, disclaim responsibility in this professional area.

This, then, is the first problem of the graduate schools—to become acquainted with what is taking place in the colleges and to reflect the knowledge of these new approaches in the curriculum provided for the prospective college and university teacher who is in pursuit of his Ph.D. degree.

In past years much has been said about the failure on the part of the universities to give the graduate student courses in professional education and experience in conducting actual classes. There is merit in this criticism. More should have been done in this area, as we shall try to make clear in a later chapter, but that shortcoming is far less serious than the failure on the part of the graduate schools to adjust their curriculum and methods to the changes that have taken place in the colleges.

Not only have the graduate schools failed in this, but in many instances they have contributed to the weaknesses of the undergraduate curriculum: the proliferation of courses in the college is traceable, in part at least, to Ph.D.'s, fresh from the graduate school, who introduce new courses in areas of their specialization. This is only natural, for the new teacher wants to share some of the insights of his graduate years with his students. Such new courses do not always contribute, however, to a well-rounded undergraduate curriculum.

No adequate criteria for the selection of subject matter have been developed. The rapid expansion of knowledge makes it imperative that some yardstick be devised for insuring that nonessential courses will not crowd out essential ones. This objective has been, in part, the motivation for the general education movement. It does not appear that the graduate schools have contributed to the achievement of this objective. Indeed, they seem to have been responsible for adding to the confusion in this area by the specialized character of the education they have provided to prospective college teachers.

The graduate schools have complained that the colleges do not prepare students properly for graduate work, and that this accounts in part for the attrition rate in graduate schools and for the delay in acquiring the doctorate. The colleges return the compliment by complaining that those who have achieved the Ph.D. are frequently so narrowly educated that they are ill prepared to impart the basic knowledge and intellectual skills necessary to a balanced and adequate undergraduate education. In short, the graduate faculties have failed to adjust their programs to the truly significant changes which are taking place in the colleges and to meet the criticism that they should vitalize and humanize their curriculums and methods of instruction.

In a real sense, the shortcomings of the college are the responsibility of the graduate schools. When the graduate program is not articulated with that of the college, there is bound to be ineffective college instruction which will, in turn, be reflected by those who seek admission to graduate schools. To put the matter in another way, the relationship of the college to the graduate school is so intimate that it is impossible to develop an effective system of higher education without the closest collaboration between the two. Such weaknesses of the college as proliferation of courses, unbalance in the curriculum, inappropriate subject matter, and the decline in the importance of the humanistic-social studies, must all be considered as largely the responsibility of the graduate schools whose product staff the college classrooms and laboratories.

One of the by-products of the lack of coordination between the college and the graduate school is confusion about the objectives of the college program. Should they include vocational as well as literary, scientific, and philosophical subjects? In some quarters the public has felt that unless college provides training for an occupation after graduation, it fails to achieve its purpose. Neither the college nor the graduate school has given effective leadership in this area. Perhaps the combined efforts of both, presenting a common front, will be required. An essential element in establishing articulation between the college and the graduate school is to insure that each is well acquainted with the purposes of the other as well as with its own.

There should also be a common understanding, too, with respect to the function of subjects in the curriculum. They were formerly spoken of as *disciplines;* for example, English, history, economics, philosophy, foreign language, and literature were styled basic disciplines. They are now frequently referred to as subject-matter areas. This apparently signifies that content has become the focus of interest. The acquisition of facts appears more important than the ability to think, learning more important than the spirit of learning, and the pursuit of knowledge a more central purpose than the pursuit of truth. This change in focus appears to apply to both undergraduate and graduate education.

Closely allied to this trend is the emphasis upon neutrality in instruction. The cult of objectivity has been dominant for many years in higher education. Some have suggested that it has produced a generation of irresponsibles. Nevertheless, the fear of substituting propaganda for education has prevailed. Perhaps it derives from the graduate school experience where subjective judgments are out of place. But more of this later.

The older college curriculum provided courses in ethics and philosophy, in history and literature, which dealt with some of the basic issues and values of human experience. The great teacher called attention to these issues and insisted upon the students' giving consideration to them. In this way a student developed a sense of values out of the mood of the discussion, the points raised by fellow students and teachers, and the general debate on the issues. To a large extent this significant sense of values has been forsaken in modern higher education in favor of a scholastic neutral education.

The social sciences deal with value systems but, in the name of objectivity, do not undertake to choose among them. Such procedure has been criticized by leading educators on both sides of the Atlantic. Sir Walter Moberly, in his *Crisis in the University*, suggested that the university no longer asks "the really fundamental questions." In the same vein, Sir Richard Livingstone remarked: "The most important task of education is to bring home to the student the greatest of all problems—the problem of living and to give him some guidance in it." "That youth needs a philosophy of living, for shaping conduct, for reference in doubt, for challenge, stimulus and driving power." An American university president sometime ago said: "What we need with an urgency beyond the power of the gravest words to reveal, is far greater wisdom and understanding to lead our generation out of the persuasion that it is adrift on seas too deep for anchorage." "I know of no more serious task for that branch of politics which we call education than to move against the spirit of fatalism which is so clearly discernible in colleges and universities."

Following a slightly different tack but emphasizing the scholastic character of present education, Arthur Bestor said in 1952: "Academic courses which teach men to perform mathematical computations but not to think mathematically, to manipulate laboratory apparatus but not to think scientifically, to remember dates but not to think historically, to summarize philosophical arguments but not to think critically—these advance no man toward liberal education."

These statements reveal the deep discontent with the impact of modern education. If we fail to ask fundamental questions, if we concentrate on knowledge rather than on understanding, if we consider only the what and the how and not the why and observe neutrality in instruction, we are unrealistic and ineffectual. The dynamic quality of education is lost if subject matter is not somehow related to life. If we know the right but have no motivation to follow it, the knowledge is of little value. In other words, it does not suffice to understand the nature of justice. Teaching that fails to inculcate a "hunger and thirst after justice," as Ruskin put it, is lacking in vitality. In short, a complete knowledge of social theory in all its aspects —economic, sociological, and political—is of little use unless it be accompanied by a sense of social responsibility. It was Aristotle who said the end of philosophy is "not knowledge but action."

President deKiewet of the University of Rochester, himself a historian, recently made this pertinent observation:

When the social sciences become merely scientific or statistical, or when the humanities become historical, they shift from their proper sphere of clarification, stimulation and advice. Any discipline which insists on being scientific or on being backward looking in the sense that the poorest forms of history are merely backward looking, becomes morally and socially neutral. At best it indicates a withdrawal of responsibility for the future, a studied neutrality towards the vital problems of humanity, a substitution of a sterile methodology for responsible thought.

In both Britain and the United States there is much concern over the future of the liberal arts. In the universities of both countries educators deplore reference to them as "service" courses. Though formerly the backbone of higher education, they seem to have lost their vitality. Since they deal with those phases of knowledge that are basic to all education, their plight may be a sinister commentary on the current state of university education.

Perhaps the reader is by now asking why such extended consideration of the problems of the liberal arts? What have they to do with graduate education? Why labor the weaknesses of the undergraduate program when discussing the needs of graduate education? First, because, as already noted, the college is suffering from lack of qualified teachers. Secondly, through the education of prospective teachers the graduate school sets the tone and spirit of the arts college. Unless there are breadth of scholarship, depth of understanding, and deep intellectual, social, and spiritual concerns in the graduate school, and unless these qualities are transmitted by that school to its students, we cannot hope to have a fully effective undergraduate program. Water cannot rise higher than its source. The source of liberal arts education is the graduate school which educates the arts college teachers. Its spirit and outlook determine the quality of the college. Perhaps this is just another way of suggesting that the weaknesses in the arts college derive from the graduate school. In the light of these facts, it is appropriate to scrutinize the college if we are to understand the graduate school. The graduate schools generally have not acknowledged this fact. Indeed, as already suggested, they have not even kept abreast of what is going on within the undergraduate institutions, if we are to judge by their programs. Instead of recognizing their responsibility to provide the leadership for improving the college, they have ignored it. It is doubtful whether they can meet their responsibility in this area under their present organization.

The greatest single need of higher education is such reforms in the graduate schools as will enable them to articulate their work with that of the colleges, that will place on them responsibility for the vitality and effectiveness of the colleges, and that will make it possible for them to assume vital leadership in American college education.

I believe this to be the future role of the graduate school. I do not believe it can be accomplished with a dean who has no authority and with a part-time faculty, such as have existed in the past and still exist. While this is not the place to discuss the organization of graduate education, it seems appropriate to suggest that the significant new role that appears to lie ahead for graduate schools may require organizational, as well as curriculum, changes. Perhaps more important still, a new outlook and sense of mission on the part of both the graduate school dean and the faculty will be needed. The graduate school has never recognized nor realized its full potential influence in American education.

The severest critic of graduate education in recent years, Earl J. McGrath, set forth his strictures on the subject in a penetrating brochure entitled "The Graduate School and the Decline of Liberal Education." He argues with great cogency and effectiveness the thesis that with the rise of graduate education, liberal education began to disintegrate, and that this occurrence was not adventitious. The specialized, analytical approach to knowledge of the graduate school, where college teachers are trained, is the opposite of the approach of the arts college; hence, the unhappy result. This has been a complaint for many years—that the specialization and fragmentation of knowledge which the graduate schools foster actually unfits one for the task of instruction in the liberal arts. Now McGrath has brought together such an array of facts and opinions of educational leaders that his indictment cannot be ignored. One cannot escape the conviction, after reading with care the impressive evidence that he submits, that our system of higher education is badly out of joint and that graduate education is the culprit. Every college and graduate school faculty member should read and ponder the facts, judgments, and conclusions of this sixty-five-page document.

One of his significant conclusions is that "only drastic reforms in graduate education will permit a much needed reorientation of liberal education" but that "before any substantial reconstruction can occur . . . the purposes of graduate education must be revised and clarified." He says further: "Until graduate faculties subject themselves to a sincere self-examination and consciously determine what they ought to be about no amelioration of the present unhappy state of affairs can be expected."[4] This is undoubtedly the hope of the future, as McGrath suggests, but would this alone solve the problem? Since the faculty is, in the main, engaged only part-time by the graduate school and since neither the graduate faculty nor the dean has authority to institute changes, it is difficult to see how the "drastic reforms" referred to could be effected.

In reviewing the discussions and criticisms of graduate education over the past twenty-five years, one is impressed with two facts. First, that no significant changes have resulted from the criticisms and, secondly, that in no instance, so far as I have observed, has the critic raised the question whether the graduate schools could, if they wished to, bring about basic changes. It seems increasingly clear that the reason why graduate schools have remained virtually unchanged in methods and procedures for more than half a century is that no one has had a primary responsibility for graduate education or authority to effect reforms, however badly they may be needed.

Another fact is equally surprising. The criticisms of the graduate schools and of the liberal arts colleges have usually stopped short of a constructive program. What should the arts and science colleges be about? The answer has been in general terms. No concrete, imaginative program has been suggested by those who lament the decline of liberal education, and no concrete changes

[4] Earl J. McGrath, *The Graduate School and the Decline of Liberal Education 1959*, p. 25.

in curriculum, methods, or procedures in the graduate school have been advanced which might give new meaning to graduate education and thereby help solve the undergraduate problems.

In the chapters that follow, in addition to calling attention to the weaknesses of the graduate schools, it will be our purpose to sketch a concrete program involving both the college and the graduate school which, it is hoped, will suggest some definite lines of action.

CHAPTER 3

Confusion in Graduate Education

It is little wonder that the situation in graduate education is clouded, since it has remained static in a sea of change for so long. But it does not mean that there is no concern. Numberless committees have studied its problems; symposiums have been conducted to consider them; elaborate statistical studies have been made in an effort to resolve the issues; and much free-lance criticism of its policies and procedures has characterized the current period. These activities reflect not only the confusion but the realization that the graduate schools have failed to meet the demands of the time.

For many years the doctor of philosophy degree has been considered the normal qualification for a teacher in colleges and universities. Yet the present annual output of the American universities supplies only about 20 per cent of the number needed to fill vacancies in the faculties of higher education. The situation appears doubly serious when one considers that college and university enrollments are expected to climb to six million by 1970, almost doubling the present number.

Despite these facts and the concern over them, there is little hope of significant change until a broad and comprehensive program has been agreed upon. The lack of such a program apparently derives from several causes. Fear of criticism, of violating sacred traditions, and of arousing antagonisms in graduate circles has inhibited a frank admission not only of the chaos and confusion that exist, but of the inadequacy that now characterizes this segment of higher education. The issues at stake are too grave to be treated with less than complete frankness and sincerity. After all, the success of graduate education is the concern not of graduate schools alone but of secondary schools, colleges, and universities—indeed, of the entire educational system. Inefficiences in these schools affect education at all levels; hence, all those interested in educational progress have a stake in seeing that they are fully effective in their operation.

To be convinced of the existing confusion, one has only to look at the roster of degrees now awarded. Originally three degrees practically made up the offerings of graduate schools—the M.A., the M.S., and the Ph.D. These still represent to many the advanced university degrees, but the two master's degrees have now proliferated into more than 150, and in addition to the Ph.D., 67 different kinds of doctorate are listed in the 1960 edition of *American Universities and Colleges*, issued by the American Council on Education. Does this multiplicity of degrees represent the higher learning in the United States? Most of them are technical, vocational, and technological degrees, such as M.S.P.H. (Master of Science in Poultry Husbandry), M.S. in Text. Mfg. (Master of Science in Textile Manufacturing), or D.M.E. (Doctor of Mechanical Engineering) and D.Agr. (Doctor of Agriculture); Doctor of Forestry has been recently added to the list of university offerings; and still more recently the degree of Doctor of Outer Space has been proposed. The growth in number of degrees has apparently more than kept pace with the expansion of knowledge. If such advanced degrees not only are included in the *higher learning* but represent the majority of those awarded, bewilderment as to its meaning is inescapable.

To add to the confusion, degrees have no uniform requirements. For instance, the M.A. in some instances requires two years of graduate work; in others, one; and in some institutions it is chiefly a fifth year of relatively poor undergraduate work. For public school teachers it is ordinarily a professional degree. The motivation in seeking it is not a scholarly interest but its dollar value. In the salary scale the M.A. holder automatically goes into a higher bracket than that of the bachelor's degree holder. It has been recently suggested that the M.A. might be awarded B.A. graduates without further study after the lapse of a period of time—a procedure sanctioned by the practices of Oxford and Cambridge and a few Indian universities. Others have proposed that the M.A. should require two full years of rigorous graduate work. How to redeem the M.A. is usually on the agenda of graduate education discussion sessions. Much is said but little is done about it. One experiment is being tried by several universities—a three-year master's degree beginning with the junior college year, about which more will be said later.

The Ph.D. serves two broad purposes: preparation for teaching in the colleges and universities, and research work in university, industrial, or independent laboratories. In most universities there is little or no recognition of this duality of purpose.

There is no common content in Ph.D. programs. For the B.A. degree certain basic subjects are usually required; for the Ph.D., none at least in some instances. This degree has been awarded to those who have written dissertations on technical or technological subjects that have no foundation in basic or pure science, much less in philosophy.

There is no time limit for securing the degree. Catalogue announcements usually prescribe a minimum of three years beyond the bachelor's degree, together with certain language requirements and a dissertation. In actual practice the lapse between the B.A. and the Ph.D. is usually seven to twelve years. On entering the graduate school, the student has no assurance that he will get a degree at all and, if he should, whether it will require three or ten years. If care is exercised in admission to the graduate school, the student should have as much assurance of receiving the Ph.D. on schedule as law or medical students have of receiving the LL.B. or M.D. in the three or four years prescribed for those degrees. The notion that the Ph.D. is *sui generis*, and should not be subject to procedures followed by other graduate degrees, is indefensible.

The character and purpose of the dissertation itself are not agreed upon. In a recent list one dissertation was 26 pages long; another, 326; and others ran as high as 1,000 pages. It is clear from an examination of the topics listed that no common agreement has been reached as to whether the dissertation should be original work, creative work, an account of research in the laboratory, a collection and organization of facts to prove a thesis, or a contribution to knowledge.

Why should such chaos prevail in what is conceded to be the most important phase of university education? The graduate faculty is usually the ablest of the university staff, the cost of graduate education is greater than any other except medical education, and the need for its products—Ph.D. graduates—is unparalleled. Yet graduate schools are more confused, ineffective, and inconsistent in their practices than any other school or college of the university. A closer look at the organization and controls of graduate education might suggest a partial answer.

What are the peculiarities of the graduate school organization that set it apart from the rest of the university? The teaching staff is borrowed from the departments of the college or professional schools. The graduate faculty member's allegiance is first to the department to which he belongs and secondarily to the graduate school. At the local level there is no one who exercises supervision over the requirements imposed by the professors on graduate students. Instances of students who have spent six to ten years writing their dissertations illustrate the point. Likewise, on the regional or national basis there is no representative group primarily concerned with graduate education. The Association of Graduate Deans of the A.A.U. is active, but it represents only about 25 per cent of the total number of institutions that grant the Ph.D. degree. They cannot, therefore, speak for graduate education nor exercise effective influence on the institutions engaged in it. Every division of higher education, except that dealing with graduate and research work, has a national organization which seeks to strengthen and promote educational programs in the area of its interest. For example, schools of law, medicine, theology, nursing, engineering, and business administration all have their national groups devoting attention to these several fields. Indeed, many departments have national organizations, such as chemistry, physics, psychology, physical education, collegiate athletics, et cetera. But in the most important single division of the university there is no organized group, representative of all the institutions that participate in graduate instruction, devoting its time and attention to the consideration of the basic problems of the graduate education enterprise.

It is not difficult to understand historically how this has come about. For the first fifty years (1876-1926) graduate work was relatively unimportant in the total university program. The *ad hoc* arrangements involving graduate committees or departments were adequate for handling the small numbers enrolled in advanced work. The flower of the *ad hoc* arrangements for handling advanced students was the graduate school with its council and its part-time faculty. The present role of the graduate school, which has the responsibility for providing the instructional staffs for colleges and universities and research staffs for business and industry, makes this informal arrangement inadequate.

It has even been suggested that the dignity of graduate education is such that it does not need to be formally organized, that it is not a professional school and must not be so considered, that it should be concerned with pure scholarship, and that, representing the apex of higher learning, it should not be expected to fit into a pattern as other divisions of the university do. In the light of the current shortage of Ph.D.'s, such attitudes are unrealistic; it is doubtful that they were ever justified.

The complacency about the failure to provide qualified staffs to man the classrooms and laboratories is disturbing. The lack of aggressive measures to recruit for graduate study, the relative indifference to the attrition rate in graduate schools, and the inordinate length of time that elapses between the B.A. and the Ph.D. reflect a laissez-faire attitude that bodes disaster if allowed to persist. Even if the value of the degree is so great that it is worth waiting for six, eight, ten, fifteen, or twenty years, society cannot afford the luxury of such a leisurely approach. The problem of adequate and qualified staffs for the colleges and universities is critical. In twenty years five generations of students pass from high school through the college to adult responsibilities.

At the 1958 meeting of the graduate deans of the A.A.U. a member reported his experience with one student, whom he termed very good, who had selected an excellent topic, and who had finally completed the work for his degree to the satisfaction of himself, his professor, and the department. The dean's account to his colleagues ran as follows: "Back of this happy catalog of items lay a rather hard experience. The dissertation was six years in the making, four of which were spent by this student teaching in a small college which, fortunately, was near by. Each time he came to talk with me I had to persuade him that he was not engaged in his life's work, and reorganize his thinking so that he would go back to the somewhat more limited problem on which he was supposed to be engaged. The first sections which he showed me were not well managed and I had to explain to him that scholarly writing did not consist of a collection of texts and footnotes. Each time, he would go home and rewrite what he had written. Nevertheless, the results in some ways justified all this effort and the student was pleased, as well as the committee. But after the examination, just as he was leaving, he said: 'I had prepared a dedication to this dissertation, but I left it out. It was to read: Dedicated to (the name of the dean) without whose understanding, encouragement and criticism this dissertation would probably have been completed five years ago.' "

The record of the meeting indicates no criticism of this procedure.

One can easily imagine how this student felt after having had to labor for six years over writing, refining, revising, and completing his dissertation. Presumably the professor might have kept him ten rather than six years rewriting and revising. The question is: Does this promote or discourage scholarly interests and productive effort? After such a long ordeal, is it not more likely that the student would be inclined never to turn his hand to writing again? It would be ironical if the most significant division of the university should be so operated as to discourage interest in scholarship rather than to develop it. Yet there is little doubt that the present method of requiring, or of allowing, seven to ten or more years for the completion of the doctor's degree does just that.

The foregoing picture of graduate education methods and procedures raises certain questions. Does the high school teacher who seeks the master's degree in order to qualify for a salary increase concentrate on subjects he is teaching, or on professional education courses that have little or no relevance to his teaching effectiveness? Why such little concern on the part of those engaged in graduate instruction over the time lag between the B.A. and Ph.D. when the deficit in fully qualified teachers is already alarming and growing each year. How much loss in teaching effectiveness was suffered by the school where the man worked for six years on his dissertation before getting it approved? What was the effect of this delay on the attitude of the student toward scholarship and research? Why do so few Ph.D. holders continue vital research after receiving the degree? Could it be that the methods of supervising dissertation writing account, in part at least, for this fact?

To shift the focus to more general considerations, let us inquire about the multiplicity of degrees (150 master's and 68 doctorates), the confusion in titles, and the variety in types of master's and doctor's degrees that are given by universities. Let us examine a few of the 150 master's degrees listed in *American Universities and Colleges* (seventh edition):

M. Prof. Acc.	Master of Professional Accountancy
M.S.G. Mgt.	Master of Science in Game Management
M.S.H.Ec.	Master of Science in Home Economics

M.S.Orn.Hort.	Master of Science in Ornamental Horticulture
M.S.P.H.	Master of Science in Public Health *or* Master of Science in Poultry Husbandry
M.S.P.H.E.	Master of Science in Public Health Engineering

Then follows a series of Master of Science degrees in textile chemistry, textile engineering, textile manufacturing, transportation, transportation engineering, retailing, paper engineering, agricultural engineering, agricultural extension, etc.

Among the doctorates recognized by the same publication are:

D.Comp.L.	Doctor of Comparative Law
D. Eng. S.	Doctor of Engineering Science
D.P.H.	Doctor of Public Health (*also* Diploma in Public Health)
D.Sc. Hyg.	Doctor of Science in Hygiene
D.S.W.	Doctor of Social Welfare
D.S.S.	Doctor of Social Science

The Doctor of Science in Hygiene is indicated by two different arrangements of the initials, D.Sc.Hyg. and Sc.D. Hyg—as if the nomenclature were not already complicated enough. Not only is there this odd variety of master's and doctor's degrees, but there are dissertations on odd subjects. Several topics picked at random will suffice to illustrate: "Participation Areas and Interest Areas in the Recreation of Students with Diverse Curriculums," "Some Distributions Related to Column Totals in Sociometric Matrices," "The Social and Psychological Setting of Communications Behavior: An Analysis of Television Viewing." The researches conducted on these topics may be of some value to someone, though this is doubtful, but a matter about which there can be little doubt is that they do not merit the award of the Ph.D. degree.

In Great Britain the colleges of advanced technology award a diploma in technology, known as the Dip. Tech., to those students who have achieved a high degree of technological competence and skill. It is not a university award nor even a degree, but it has high standing because of the quality of training it requires. Perhaps the atmosphere in American universities could be cleared if some sort of technological award were made for technical or technological studies of high quality. By no stretch of the imagination can the Ph.D. be awarded appropriately for such work. The accrediting associations will not permit the B.A. degree to be awarded for a program that does not include basic subject matter, but there is no organization operative in the graduate field which exercises such a restraining influence.

It may be that universities can appropriately engage in developing technologists. No other educational institutions are equipped to do it, but the degree awarded for such training should be appropriately labeled. It surely is not appropriate to award the Ph.D. for a dissertation on "Approximate Elastic Analysis of Slabs with Openings" or on "Instrumentation for Locating and Identifying Noises in Mechanical Equipment." These are dissertation topics used by successful doctoral candidates. While a Master of Technology might be appropriate in these two cases, it is more difficult to classify the following: A private university granted the doctor's degree to a young woman who wrote her dissertation on the "Effects of Stress on College Women in Situations Involving Competition." Another private university on the East Coast awarded the Ph.D. for a dissertation 217 pages long on "A Study of Some Factors in the Written Language of a Group of Texas Land-Grant College Freshmen to Show How the Nature of the Language Reflects the Socio-Economic Backgrounds of These Students." Another land-grant college granted the doctorate to a student whose dissertation subject was "Organizational Relationships of the Office Manager"; it took 326 pages to tell the story.

Perhaps it would be of interest to list without comment a few additional dissertation subjects used for doctorates:

A land-grant college   "The Rank Analysis of Triple Comparisons" (125 pages)

A state university	"The Flame Spectrophotometric Determination of Magnesium" (217 pages)
A state university	"An Evaluation of the Undergraduate Professional Preparation in Physical Education for Men in Selected Colleges and Universities in Indiana" (234 pages)
A state university	"Flows of Isometries" (46 pages)
A land-grant college	"A Study of a Basic Set of Polyharmonic Polynomials" (26 pages)

Of the twelve institutions represented by the dissertation topics discussed and listed above, the majority are members of the American Association of Universities; some have only recently inaugurated the Ph.D., while others have had some years' experience with advanced graduate work, though they are not members of the A.A.U.

If graduate schools in the United States award the highest academic distinction for essentially trivial researches in technical and vocational subjects, it is fair to conclude that graduate education is either seriously confused or so unorganized that indefensible practices can be engaged in without restraint. It is clear that the stronger universities would not condone some of these practices, but there is no means of remedying the situation until some changes in the organization of graduate education have been effected.

The question is not whether a specific dissertation has value, but whether, even though it is appropriate for practical research, it belongs in a university, and particularly whether it is of such quality as to warrant the award of the Doctor of Philosophy degree. If research is on basic scientific subjects, the Ph.D. would certainly be an appropriate recognition; but when it is on a subject that is wholly in an applied science area and, as in some cases, deals with rather superficial aspects of that area, it is difficult to justify. But the record is clear: it has occurred in a considerable number of institutions and is still occurring.

Those who are inclined to scoff at the need for better organization of graduate schools and graduate work generally, should take note of these vagaries in the award of the highest academic degree. The notion that graduate education does not need more systematic planning and that its leaders have ample authority to achieve their purposes does not appear justified in the light of these facts. If we are to meet the needs of the colleges and universities for well-qualified instructional personnel, more attention must be focused on vigorous recruitment and graduate instruction and on effective articulation of college and university programs, to the end of providing men and women in sufficient numbers and with appropriate training to man the classrooms and laboratories of the universities and the laboratories of industry.

The institutions that awarded the Ph.D. for the dissertations listed on pages 73-74 are located in all sections of the country; they are of all types—public and private; and all the degrees involving these dissertations have been awarded in the past four years. The Northeast, the Middle Atlantic states, the Southeast, the Midwest, the Far West—all are represented in the list. State universities, land-grant colleges, private universities, and municipal universities—large and small—are among the number.

The graduate schools of the country cannot afford to be indifferent to the nature of the research for which the highest academic degree is awarded. Some graduate school accepted each of the dissertations listed, on the basis of which the Ph.D. was granted; each topic was selected or approved by an individual faculty member. The graduate school apparently does not assume responsibility for the topics that departments approve. Its lack of responsibility in an area so vital to the soundness of higher education is a matter of genuine concern, since the tone and the quality of graduate education are involved. If each professor in the graduate school is sovereign in his field, and no one dares to invade his sovereignty, this may account for the prevailing chaos. Surely the time has come for a reorganization of graduate education. Graduate schools of the country cannot escape responsibility for the vagaries of current procedures in universities that award the Ph.D. Some organization that would enable the stronger graduate schools to set policies and to exercise supervision over practices would seem to be imperative if the quality of the Ph.D. is to be safeguarded.

Such an organization should inquire into the reasons for and the meaning of the multiplicity and confusion of graduate degrees, with a view to arriving at some common conception of the aims and functions of graduate education. It should be able to resolve the issue respecting the most appropriate means of combining preparation for college and university teaching with scholarship in the Ph.D. program. Since the highest scholarship is the best training for those who are to teach college and university youth, scholarship and professional preparation at this level should not be antithetical. Other matters that such an organization should consider are: (1) the means of insuring the quality of the M.A. and the Ph.D.; (2) a plan for distinguishing between technical and graduate degrees; (3) the elimination of subject matter inappropriate to university graduate programs; (4) reduction in number of degrees; (5) clarification of terminology in cases where there is a double meaning, and where the same degree has different designations: for instance, Master of Science—M.S. and Sc.M.; Master of Laws—M.L. and LL.M.; Master of Landscape Architecture—M.L.A. and M.L. Arch.

The useless multiplication of advanced degrees and the confusion with respect to them could presumably be eliminated without great difficulty by an organization representative of all universities engaged in advanced graduate work. Though many of the degrees referred to are awarded for work done in professional schools, it would seem logical for the graduate schools to take the initiative in working out needed improvements in the area of post-college work, particularly since professional schools are frequently represented on the graduate faculties through their graduate course teachers.

The terminology used to designate achievements in this area has grown like Topsy. No one has planned it. No one has controlled it. No one has attempted to limit it. Each institution has followed its own inclinations. It is not unlikely that universities, including their professional schools, would welcome a constructive effort on the part of the graduate school leadership to clarify and simplify the degree structure. No more appropriate time for such a move could be found than in the nineteen-sixties, on the eve of the greatest expansion of advanced work yet experienced.

The public has a right to expect more consistency and less confusion than is manifest in the 150 master's and 68 doctor's degrees currently listed in college and university catalogues. As higher education becomes more dependent upon public funds, closer scrutiny of programs as well as of expenditures will naturally result. Educational institutions cannot afford to ignore this fact. The universities cannot justify the present confusion. Failure to meet their obligation to restore order and meaning in this area might jeopardize their autonomy and end in their forfeiting some of the privileges that have traditionally been considered essential to their proper functioning.

Over and above the unwarranted proliferation of degrees, the confusion with respect to the M.A. and the Ph.D., the length of time required for the Ph.D., the dual purposes it is designed to serve, the lack of definite goals, the criticisms of the dissertations, the examinations, etc., still another problem confronts graduate education that has been largely overlooked: it is the uneven distribution of doctorates in the several fields of knowledge.

The shortage of Ph.D.'s in science is widely publicized, but that in other areas is little known. For example, in 1958 two and one half times more doctorates were awarded in education than in economics, history, English, classical languages, and political science combined. In the study of baccalaureate origins of doctorates in the humanities and social sciences, conducted by the American Academy of Sciences, the number of doctor's degrees in education, sociology, and psychology during the period from 1936 to 1950 was almost equal to that in all other subjects, excluding the natural sciences. There is a growing shortage of staff in the humanistic-social studies field. The country, therefore, needs not only strong, well-organized, and well-managed graduate schools but a better balanced distribution of graduate students. To achieve this result will require careful planning and a comprehensive effort on the part of colleges and universities. Again, the leadership of the graduate schools will be of central importance.

Changes in graduate education organization and control will be required before the graduate schools can hope to perform effectively the functions that can scarcely be performed by any other segment of the university. Graduate deans have expressed opposition to the idea of a separate graduate faculty, on the ground that the present organization gives them all the authority needed for administering the graduate program. While this may be true so far as the routine operation of the enterprise is concerned, the arrangement still does not provide a faculty who can give undivided attention to the needs of graduate education as a whole, studying such matters as the changes in policy and practice that may be required before the deficit in qualified instructional manpower can be met, the elimination of the indefensible procedures found in some institutions, improvement in the quality of the Ph.D., and how to reduce the attrition rate and shorten the time lag between the B.A. and the Ph.D.

The late Dr. Jessup, in his last report as president of the Carnegie Foundation for the Advancement of Teaching, wrote: "The graduate school, long torpid, may be on the brink of movement. As yet it has merely stirred in its sleep. If there is to be a true awakening, there must be action."[1] Sixteen years have elapsed since that startling description of the graduate school was penned by an experienced university and foundation executive who was also a close student of American education.

What has happened during the past decade and a half? Though the number of graduate students has increased substantially and many institutions have inaugurated the Ph.D. program during that period, no significant changes in operation,

---

[1] Carnegie Foundation for the Advancement of Teaching, *Annual Report* (1943-4), p. 3.

in control, in requirements, in curriculum, in methods, or in effectiveness are recorded. Indeed, the gap between the supply and the demand for Ph.D.'s is the widest in the history of graduate education. No "action" has been taken to indicate that "a true awakening" has occurred. Scattered, sporadic efforts have been made in some quarters, but in the main the graduate school is still in "business as usual."

A careful study of these facts indicates that the reasons for the resistance to change appear to inhere in the nature of the organization of graduate education. No farflung and growing enterprise can prosper if its branch managers have no authority; if the chief officers of each unit are borrowed from other agencies which can claim their first allegiance; if no one is concentrating on its welfare and dedicating his full energies to its service; and if there is no organization representing all of its branches, which can speak for it and exercise at least a coordinating influence over the several branches. All these defects are found in the organization of graduate education.

It is certainly a farflung and growing enterprise, with its 160 institutions giving the Ph.D. and many more awarding the M.A. The heads of the units (graduate deans) have no authority over their chief officers (faculty members), who are beholden to their department heads rather than to the graduate school executive and who cannot, therefore, give undivided attention to advanced work. Finally, there is no association, representative of all graduate schools, concerned about the effectiveness and progress of graduate education and devoting its efforts to the improvement of the national program.

The graduate deans' reluctance to advocate a plan that would give them individually and collectively greater authority is understandable. It might subject them to the criticism that their object was empire building. For that reason, the initiative in undertaking graduate school reorganization will have to come from the central administration. The provost or the academic vice-president could appropriately be given the authority and responsibility for taking the lead on the campus. In a matter so vital to all higher education, the board of trustees has both the right and the obligation to take a deep interest and to give its encouragement to changes looking to greater efficiency in this strategic division of the university.

In view of the critical shortage of qualified teachers in colleges and universities, it is imperative that steps be taken to increase the output. Despite the Woodrow Wilson and the National Defense Education Act fellowships and the many other efforts to increase the flow of trained teachers, the supply is far from adequate. Additional funds are needed, but more than that will be required. The graduate schools must be geared to more efficient handling of their students as well as to more aggressive recruitment.

Everyone is agreed that seven to twelve years should not be required for the average graduate student to proceed from the B.A. to the Ph.D. The program should be more definite, more rigorous, and more systematic. For a good student with a good subject to be required to spend six years producing a dissertation, as in the case reported to the A.A.U. deans, makes no sense. In a properly organized and efficient graduate school such a procedure would not be tolerated, and yet under the present plan it is not possible to prevent it. The graduate professor may hold up the completion of the thesis for ten years or, if he chooses, refuse approval altogether without consultation with his colleagues on the faculty. If the graduate dean does not approve such action, the professor may simply decline to give further graduate courses, and no one can gainsay it. While such action may occur only very rarely, an organization that permits it cannot be justified. In the present crisis and in view of the current confusion, it is of crucial importance that the graduate school have more effective controls. The nature of the present arrangement, as its history indicates, discourages attempts at significant changes.

With such a relationship between the graduate faculty and the dean, it follows that neither can be expected to feel a primary responsibility to study systematically, with a view to action, the needs of graduate education. By the same token, both would feel presumptuous in suggesting basic changes in policy and practices since this would imply dissatisfaction with the present arrangements. To criticize a colleague for his handling of graduate students would be *ultra vires* under the present framework.

In the light of these facts, it is not difficult to understand why graduate schools have failed to make the progress expected of them. They have been, and still are, practically helpless to achieve basic changes in organization, procedure, curriculum, methods, or goals because of the nature of their organization and the dependent relationship between them and other divisions of the universities. They are victims of an organizational structure that stifles initiative, violates sound principles of administration, and cripples them by failing to give proper status to administrative and teaching staffs, upon whom rests the responsibility of conducting their program in the businesslike manner that characterizes other divisions of the universities.

The suggestion that the graduate school is so different in educational function from other divisions of the university that it does not need the same administrative organization and controls makes no sense. After all, its personnel belong also to other divisions of the university which are fully organized. At best, such a suggestion seems little more than an attempt to rationalize the status quo.

The President of the Carnegie Corporation in his 1938 annual report had this to say:

For long years, the graduate school, its mysteries culminating in the rites and ceremonials attending the award of the Ph.D. degree, has been the sacred cow in American education, to be worshipped rather than studied, understood and improved. As a vested interest, it has demanded and received without question financial support beyond that provided for any other branch of learning, with the single exception of modern medicine.[2]

Following these statements the late Dr. Keppel proceeded to ask a series of questions which are still pertinent twenty-three years later.

[2] Carnegie Corporation, of New York, *Report of the President and of the Treasurer* (1938), pp. 35-6.

What are these schools really doing? What kind of students are they attracting, and how intelligently and realistically are they dealing with them when drawn into the net? Is the current pattern of classroom and laboratory courses, which the graduate school years ago took over bodily from the undergraduate college, the most efficient or even the cheapest way to meet its own particular needs? Regardless of their public professions to the contrary, have they become primarily vocational institutions? Are their thoughts concerned chiefly with providing the labels demanded of college teachers and, to an increasing degree, of all teachers, and secondarily with preparing students to fill positions in industry and technology, for which our engineering and other specialized colleges do not make satisfactory provisions?[3]

These basic questions still need answering. Only the graduate school can answer them.

[3] *Ibid.*, p. 36.

CHAPTER 4

Science, Technology,
and the University Tradition

One of the most difficult adjustments required of university education has been that of fitting the scientific approach to learning into the framework of the historical and traditional modes of thinking and instructional practices inherited from the Middle Ages. The empirical method of arriving at the truth contrasted sharply with a priori deductive logic. The dialectical method of instruction has little in common with the laboratory experiment. The great contribution of the Rennaissance was the introduction of empiricism as a method of advancing knowledge.

Its effect in the area of practical affairs was much more immediate than its influence on university education, as the industrial revolution of the nineteenth century suggests. Science and particularly technology were late comers in the curriculums of universities. Even after their arrival they did not affect university life significantly until long after they had been grudgingly accorded a place in the higher learning. It is only within recent decades that they have gained such a position of prestige and prominence as to raise questions about their effect on the nature, the goals, and the spirit of university education.

Since research in science and technology has profoundly influenced modern research in the humanistic-social science fields and currently receives the lion's share of research budgets, it has seemed important to sketch an outline of the background of university education, with special reference to the kinds of problems that have arisen in connection with efforts to adjust the new curriculums and new methods to the university tradition, which was already some seven centuries old before science and technology were accepted as appropriate subjects of study for university students. Such an outline may be useful not only in providing perspective, as we consider graduate studies in general, but also in throwing light on the problems peculiar to the humanities and the social sciences.

Every age and every country shapes its own educational system. The prevailing social, economic, and political philosophies play a dominant role in its development. Likewise, the discovery of new knowledge and the emergence of new needs affect the pattern. In times of social revolution university changes are accelerated. But during its eight-hundred-year history the university has also established certain traditions and goals that are common to all, pursuit of truth, knowledge for its own sake, free inquiry, search for reality—the *summum bonum.*

Since their beginning universities have been concerned with a wide variety of intellectual fields, in differing communities and under varying legal institutions. They are now, as in the past, associated with scholarship, philosophies of life, educational systems, professional training; with church and state, law and finance; and in recent times with interest in technical progress and economic systems.

Since many of the early institutions were given authority to grant degress by the Pope, they considered themselves Church institutions. The religious atmosphere and aspirations in the early days were marked characteristics of these institutions. At the same time they were established as self-governing by secular authority, with their own courts and finances, and were generally exempt from taxation. Thus, both Church and State have exercised a major influence over the spirit and fortunes of universities as social institutions.

As teaching institutions they have provided instruction in a wide variety of fields. Gradually the curriculum became stabilized with four main faculties—theology, law, medicine, and the arts. The faculty of arts was designed to prepare students for the higher studies which were the learned professions. This faculty taught the liberal arts, the trivium and the quadrivium, and the philosophy of Aristotle until the Renaissance.

Humanism and the great intellectual and social upheaval known as the Renaissance, brought about substantial changes in the content of the higher learning, particularly in the area of the faculty of arts. Ancient languages were added to the curriculum—Latin, Greek, Hebrew—for they were the keys to the knowledge found in the newly discovered Latin, Greek, and Hebrew classics. The new body of history, philosophy, and literature embodied in these ancient papyri, gradually became subjects of study. The poetry and drama of Greece, the military history and legal systems of Rome, and the religious history and philosophy of the Hebrews were introduced into the arts faculty. Roman law was studied alongside canon law, the Hippocratic (Greek) collection was studied in preparation for medical practice, and so on. Through the influence of other intellectual movements of a similar kind, universities were gradually secularized and emancipated from Church control.

In the beginning the development of technology and the natural sciences was largely achieved outside the universities by individual scholars and scientists through personal exchange of ideas and the establishment of learned societies, such as the Royal Society of London and similar ones in Italy, France, and Germany. Universities were institutions for professional training, the faculty of philosophy remaining as a preparatory step for the higher studies. Its subjects included traditional studies of the arts and Aristotelian philosophy along with lectures in classical languages and literature, leaving development in the sciences to creative, scientific-minded scholars outside the university.

Technology as well as science arose without benefit of the university. The higher technical studies developed for utilitarian reasons during the industrial revolution, which was itself the result of numerous scientific discoveries and inventions. They were in no way connected with theology, and as they frequently were contrary to the dogmatic teachings of the Church, they were thought to engender heretical views. In some cases in England fanatical mobs destroyed the new institutions and their laboratories. Partly for this reason the higher technical educational agencies developed apart from the universities, supported by individuals, private groups, or secular governments. Sometimes they were established by rulers as state institutions and supported entirely by public funds. Since such institutions could not attain the semi-independent position of the universities, they thus remained notably inferior in academic status. It was not until the twentieth century that they began to be fully recognized by the universities. Now many of the new technological faculties—engineering, agriculture, mining, and commerce—are incorporated as integral divisions of universities and have in recent years been developing advanced degrees to a marked extent.

The University of London was the first British university to establish undergraduate work in engineering. Its King's College created a chair of engineering in 1838; its University College, civil engineering in 1841 and mechanical in 1846. It was not until 1878 that Cambridge established a faculty of engineering. Technological studies in Britain developed slowly in the universities partly because of their high cost.

The demand for government help in developing such programs in the late nineteenth and early twentieth centuries resulted in the establishment of the British University Grants Committee (U.G.C.) in 1919. This committee was designed to systematize the making of Treasury grants and to aid in the development of university programs, with particular reference to science and technology. From 1919 to 1939 the growth of government grants was slow, increasing from £900,000, in round figures, in 1919, to £2,224,000 in 1939. The annual grants remained at that figure during the war. Since 1946, however, the growth of Treasury support has skyrocketed, to approximately £39,500,-000 by 1962, under the current quinquennium plan. In addition, some £70,000,000 were earmarked for buildings and equipment during the 1957-to-1962 period.

In the United States the real beginning of the development of science and technology was the Land-Grant College Act of 1862. The struggle to gain acceptance for these institutions and for their technological studies was long and discouraging. Forty years after the passage of the legislation creating the land-grant colleges, science and technology were still not generally popular, though the government had increased its support of the institutions and provided funds for expanding their programs. Since 1900 the growth of interest in these subjects has been phenomenal. Not only land-grant colleges but state universities, privately supported colleges and universities, and technological institutes provide instruction in these fields.

Research has become a major industry. Not only universities but government, business, and industry give it a high priority. The annual budget for research in the United States is some sixteen billion dollars, of which nine billion comes from government and seven billion from business and industry. This places upon the universities the responsibility for training the scientists and the technologists. The demand for these trainees is so great that educational institutions find it difficult to retain a sufficient number to man their classrooms and laboratories. Even so, industry is forced to train much of its research personnel after taking all the university graduates available.

The overwhelming need for scientists and technologists in both Britain and the United States results in a variety of efforts to recruit them. In the United States, government, industry, and private agencies provide scholarships, fellowships, and other inducements. In Britain during the current quinquennium, 1957 to 1962, the U.G.C. suggested that two thirds of the increase in number of students planned for should be enrolled in science and technology subjects, and the funds for buildings and equipment are earmarked for scientific and technological facilities. This does not take into account the sums expended for technical colleges, the colleges of advanced technology, and other non-university institutions in Britain. In both the United States and Britain one frequently hears the complaint that the college of arts and sciences has become merely a service division, rather than the central core of basic studies serving as the foundation for an effective university.

These facts have basic implications for higher education. It would appear, first of all, that the curriculum is out of balance, due to the heavy emphasis on science and technology, but more disturbing than that is the threat to university integrity. What happens to the ideal of knowledge for its own sake, to "pursuit of truth" as the purpose of university education, and to the goal of individual development of students.

The emphasis on science and technology is practical, owing to economic and defense needs. Knowledge for its own sake is replaced by knowledge for the sake of its returns to society. Pursuit of truth now becomes, too largely, pursuit of facts relevant to particular needs. The goals of intellectual development, growth of personality, and character building seem now to be largely replaced by the goal of producing the maximum number of units of skilled manpower—scientists and technologists. Filling the needs of society has apparently become more important than meeting the needs of the individual. Obviously there is, and always has been, an overlap between these two purposes. It might be argued that the needs of society can in the long run best be met by providing for the needs of the individual. It is less certain that meeting the needs of society, which fluctuate from decade to decade, will best provide for the long-range needs of either it or the individual.

Few would argue seriously that emphasis upon scientific and technological studies is out of place in these times. It is essential for survival, but it may also be essential to survival that basic studies be emphasized. It is undoubtedly important for the research specialist to have some knowledge of his heritage and of the social forces at work in his society. Otherwise he cannot become properly oriented to it; and, in view of his strategic role in modern society, he must be not only informed but attuned

to what is going on in it. On the other hand, it is just as important for the arts student, the one who takes humanistic-social
studies as his major interest, to know something about the role
of science and technology in our society.

Every university graduate should certainly have some knowledge of science and some understanding of the social implications of technology. It is an indispensable part of his orientation
to the world in which he lives. And yet in many Commonwealth
universities those pursuing the B.A. in the humanities have no
opportunity to study science or the scientific method. It appears
strange that in this atomic age vast numbers of university graduates with B.A. degrees should have had no university assistance
in understanding science and technology, their role in the
modern world, and their influence on social change. By the same
token, it is equally difficult to rationalize leaving out of the educational menu of science students those courses of study that
would help them understand the background of their society
and its structure. This is not only a scientific and technological
but also an ideological age. New political and economic theories
have flourished in this century as in few other periods of history.
The ideals of democracy and freedom, of human dignity and
inalienable rights, and of respect for religion and social justice
have been attacked more vigorously and brutally in the past few
decades than ever before in modern times. In such a situation it
is difficult to justify an educational system that produces university graduates who have no real acquaintance with the social,
economic, and political philosophies upon which their culture
rests.

In short, undergraduate programs of the future must somehow provide a more balanced educational diet if they are to
succeed in producing wise and intelligent leadership. In English
universities, and in some of their offspring in the Commonwealth
countries, basic curriculum reforms will be necessary to achieve
such a balanced program. In Scottish, Canadian, and American
universities, which have recognized the principle in their arts
and science college curriculums, more realistic efforts will be

needed before a really satisfactory program is developed. Neither the arts faculties in Commonwealth countries nor the arts and science colleges in Canada and the United States appear to have conceived clearly the basic function of the humanistic-social studies, much less devised an adequate curriculum.

The confusion as to the purpose of humanistic education has been responsible, in part at least, for its present unhappy plight. The notion that it is a cultural course in the narrow sense, designed to adorn its possessor with polish, refinement, and distinction, has maligned its purpose and distorted its value. Unless it assists in giving one a realistic understanding of his heritage, of his physical, social, and biological environment, and of himself, it has failed to achieve its objective. Such an understanding is essential to intelligent citizenship. While this is the broad purpose of arts and science colleges, neither the curriculum nor the focus of instruction are in many instances realistically designed to achieve it.

The objectives of the undergraduate programs in all the universities of the Commonwealth and the United States need clarification followed by curriculum revisions. This is the task of universities under the leadership of their graduate faculties. New courses, new methods of instruction, and adaptation to technological and professional programs will be required, and it is important that they be undertaken by the university staffs rather than risk non-university handling of the matter.

The suggestion that changes should be made in the curriculum raises the question of what kind of humanistic-social studies students of science and technology need. Sir Eric Ashby, formerly vice-chancellor of Queen's University in Belfast and now head of Clare College, Cambridge, recently made a notable statement stressing the importance of these studies for the scientist and the technologist and outlining specifically what should be required. He said:

First, they should not include subjects which can, and ought to be taught in school. They should be taught as genuine humanities [dealing with] the creative and social acts of man and particularly with value judgments, ideas of right and wrong, of good and evil, of justice, freedom and government, in such a way as to be relevant to the contemporary world and to technology [and as] instruments to enhance the individuality of students to resist that levelling of differences in taste and personality [which tends to result from the modern techniques of mass communication].[1]

Not only is this analysis a valuable contribution to contemporary thought on a subject of central importance, but it is significant as an indication of the concern of certain British leaders over this matter. Indeed, it is a deep concern throughout the university world. How to blend the humanistic-social studies with the program in science and technology in such way as to produce both the most effective citizen and the most effective scientists and technologists remains an unsolved problem.

A few years ago the Canadian Commission on National Development in Arts, Letters, and Science summed up its view in the following statement: "Humanistic studies do not belong only to the faculty of liberal arts but should pervade the professional schools as well. They should permeate the entire university. A professional school without the humanities is little more than a technical institute."[2]

In November 1957 the Prime Minister of Australia, Mr. Menzies urged the importance of humanistic studies, saying:

But I hope that we will not under current pressures or emotions be tempted to ignore the basic fact that civilization, in the true sense, requires a close and growing attention not only to science and all its branches but also to those studies of the mind and spirit of man, of history and literature and language, and mental and moral philosophy, of human relations in society and industry, of international understanding, the relative neglect of which has left a gruesome mark on this century.

Let us have more scientists and more humanists. Let the scientists be touched and informed by the humanities. Let the humanists be touched and informed by science so that they may not be lost in the abstractions derived from outdated knowledge or circumstances. That proposition underlies the whole university idea. It warrants and requires a great variety

---

[1] Statement by Sir Eric Ashby, *Technology and the Academics*, pp. 85-6.
[2] Statement, Canadian Commission on National Development in Arts, Letters, and Science, pp. 135-6.

of faculties and the constant intermingling of those who are engaged in their disciplines.[3]

In 1956 a British educationist pointed out that in Russia about one eighth of the curriculum in the technological institutes is devoted to the humanities and the social sciences, and said: "If Russia thinks it worthwhile to make technological students spend one-eighth of their time on literature and history and economics and to pass examinations on these subjects, we should, at least, examine the proposition closely."[4]

Perhaps the best way to express the American point of view would be to quote from a recent bulletin of the Massachusetts Institute of Technology. It sets forth the purposes of this institution in the following language:

> In attaining its present position the Institute has constantly kept before it three objectives—the education of men, the advancement of knowledge and the rendering of service to industry and the nation. It aims to give its students such a combination of humanistic, scientific and professional training as will fit them to take leading positions in a world in which science, engineering and architecture are of basic importance. This training is especially planned to prepare students according to their desires and aptitudes to become practicing engineers or architects, investigators, business executives, or teachers. The useful knowledge and mental discipline gained in this training are, however, so broad and fundamental as to constitute an excellent general preparation for other courses.[5]

Adjustment of science and technology programs to the university tradition is one of the basic problems of modern higher learning. The solution will require the dedicated efforts of our ablest scholars and scientists, using their knowledge and skill in research as well as their wisdom. This appears again to be another task for the leaders in graduate education.

Science and technology are but one facet of a larger problem, that of the proliferation of professional and semiprofessional

[3] Statement by Robert Gordon Menzies in the House of Representatives (November 1957).

[4] Statement of a British educationist at a meeting of the Home Universities Conference (1956).

[5] Bulletin, Massachusetts Institute of Technology.

courses in the university curriculum. No one would question the appropriateness of preparation for the learned professions in the university. Many of the older European universities began as faculties of law, medicine, or theology, or some combination of these. What does concern thoughtful students of university education is the multiplication of professional or vocational curriculums that seek university sponsorship.

The latest *American Universities and Colleges* (1960) lists twenty-two occupations for which American colleges and universities provide preparation. In the light of university traditions and ideals, some people would consider it difficult to rank optometry, osteopathy, and certain phases of agriculture as worthy of university status. At a recent national meeting on higher education a graduate dean suggested that psychology, chemistry, and other subjects seemed to be moving toward the establishment of separate schools. Apart from particular courses that seem to be misfits in a university curriculum and apart from unwarranted fragmentation, the fact that so large a proportion of university work is in technical and professional fields is a matter of concern to the future of university education. So much of it involves skills rather than intellectual effort, acquisition of information rather than intellectual initiative, and consideration of secondary facts rather than basic principles.

Our age is given not to meditation and reflection but to action. Our educational systems reflect that fact in their emphasis on science and technology. Much of the research undertaken, the effort to push back the frontiers of knowledge, is done under contract. The object is restricted, and the findings must be relevant to a predetermined purpose: otherwise they do not serve the interests of the patron. Free-ranging research, in the pursuit of knowledge for its own sake, seems on the way to becoming obsolete in some institutions of higher learning. Support for basic investigation is meager; for applied research, abundant. The tendency of the times is to insist upon prompt and pragmatic results. A sense of urgency tends to discourage pure research and scholarship. Business, industry, and government are spending fantastic sums for *ad hoc* research but little for basic investigation.

The present extent of the universities' acceptance of applied research contracts suggests one aspect of the problem of adjustment that the emphasis on science and technology imposes on higher education. This is, however, only a relatively minor one. The effect of the method and the philosophy of research in the natural sciences, which have influenced the research approach of scholars in the humanities and social science fields, constitutes the basic issue in the adjustment.

In the natural sciences a body of knowledge has been built up on a foundation of accepted assumptions, concepts, and demonstrated facts; in the humanistic-social studies no such substructure exists. Moreover, in the humanities values, not facts, are the essential elements. The scientific approach employed in this area may arrive at some facts *about* languages, literature, history, and philosophy but will not discover their essence, their values, without which they have little or no meaning. The dictionary defines the humanities as "the branches of learning concerned with human thought and relations, as distinguished from the sciences." Their subject matter, their purpose, and their contribution to human progress are unlike those of the sciences, and yet the humanistic scholars have never developed a research rationale appropriate to their subject matters. They have instead adopted the methods of the natural sciences, which has been responsible for all kinds of confusion as well as ineffectiveness in research results.

Social scientists have also followed the lead of the natural scientists. The dictionary definition of social science is "the study of people and *how* they live together as families, tribes, communities, races, etc." It deals "with the structure of society and the activity of its members." It has produced many facts *about* society but little knowledge *of* society. It has developed a body of knowledge of *how* people live together but provides no understanding of *why* they behave as they do. In the natural sciences it is not important to know why two atoms of hydrogen get together with one of oxygen to form a molecule of water; it is only necessary to know that they do. In the field of human relations the important consideration is the reason for individual or collective action—the circumstances, the ideas, the concepts and the ideals which underlie behavior.

In other words, an understanding of physics and chemistry involves knowledge of the reactions of physical and chemical elements under given conditions. But human beings have no such fixed reactions; their responses are determined by their motivations, which are based upon their scale of values. Hence, social research designed to improve society must of necessity deal with unseen and unpredictable forces, with ideas, ideals, aspirations, hopes, and fears. In short, the methods of research that achieve results in the natural sciences will not suffice in the area of human relations. Social institutions do not arise spontaneously when people live together in communities; they spring from human desires and hopes. Hence, a study that confines itself to learning *about* institutions may be useful in cataloging them but not in understanding them, except as social phenomena. To know them and to understand their significance it is necessary to be acquainted with the forces that brought them into being. To know the *structure* of society is not synonymous with understanding *society*. For that reason, research concerned with "*how* people live together" is inadequate.

Another difficulty in the areas of the social sciences and the humanities is the inadequacy of the substructure of knowledge on which to build a truly scientific superstructure. It was a long while before natural philosophy developed into the natural sciences. Long and patient labors were required before a science of physics, chemistry, or biology could be born. Painstaking efforts to build up the basic knowledge to serve as a foundation in each of the sciences was followed by the task of arranging systematically all the facts discovered, the concepts developed, and the principles formulated. The social sciences were the offspring of moral philosophy—just as the physical and biological sciences were of natural philosophy—but they have not developed similar solid foundations of assumptions, concepts, and demonstrated facts.

Further discussion of the problems of graduate and research work in the humanities and social sciences will be reserved for later chapters. They have been touched upon briefly here only to point out certain aspects of the difficulty of fitting science and technology into the traditional university program.

CHAPTER 5

Graduate Education
in the Humanities

Criticisms of the graduate school center chiefly around the humanities and social sciences. In the natural sciences there is less dissatisfaction. The student moves much more rapidly toward the Ph.D. On the average the lag between the B.A. and the Ph.D. in the natural sciences is only a little more than a half that in some humanistic subjects. The usual explanation is that the monetary rewards of the Ph.D. in chemistry or physics are so much greater than those of the English or history Ph.D. that there is a correspondingly greater incentive. A brief analysis of this commonly accepted view will readily reveal its weakness.

The doctorate is far less a requirement for scientific and industrial research workers than for college and university teachers. Among business and industrial employers the advanced degree is rarely a *sine qua non* of employment, whereas in the university world it is for anyone who aspires to be more than a second-class professor. In monetary, as well as in prestige, terms the doctorate is essential. The fetish of the Ph.D. in college and university circles is well known and frequently deplored. In many institutions a full professorship is rarely, if ever, awarded a teacher, however effective he may be in the classroom, if he does not have maximum training. The incentive, therefore, for one who seeks a career in higher education is impelling, far more so than for one who aspires to be an industrial chemist or physicist.

What, then, is the difference between the sciences and the

77

humanities that results in the lag between the B.A. and the Ph.D. being seven years in the former and twelve in the latter? To one who has observed the situation closely and over a long period, the difference appears fairly clear. Graduate school methods are well adapted to the physical and biological sciences but unsuited, in essential ways, when applied literally to the literary, historical, and philosophical areas. Since the sciences deal primarily with facts, research has a clear purpose to find the facts necessary to prove or disprove an hypothesis. The humanities traditionally are, and properly should be, concerned with ideas, concepts, and values. McGrath summed it up in a sentence: "With the rise of the graduate school liberal education became oriented toward new goals foreign to its nature."[1]

He elaborated:

Under the spreading influence of graduate education, the liberal arts colleges shifted their interest from teaching to research; from instruction concerned with the key ideas of Western culture to instruction composed of the latest findings in ever narrower areas of scholarly investigation; from a concern with the complete development of mind and character—to the cultivation of the professional skills and the restricted subject matter of the various fields of intellectual endeavor.[2]

To some areas, such as linguistics, the method employed in natural science research is well adapted. Linguistics is the science of language embracing syntax, morphology, phonology and semantics, structure and development. In its general aspects it is subdivided into historical, geographical, comparative, and descriptive linguistics. The analytical approach, involving a painstaking search for facts, is logical and effective. Here is a subject, incorporated in the humanities, that is a *science* and, therefore, responds well to the scientific method. The popularity of linguistics among humanistic scholars may derive largely from this fact. The objective can be clearly stated, and the progress toward achieving it can be easily measured. Linguistics is the scientific treatment of a humanistic subject, just as teaching

---

[1] Earl J. McGrath, *The Graduate School and the Decline of Liberal Education*, Bureau of Publications, Teachers College, Columbia University, p. 14.
[2] *Ibid.*, pp. 14-15.

science to non-science majors should be a humanistic treatment of science.

All would agree that science instruction is more than teaching about science; otherwise there would be no need for laboratories. Scientific research is more than investigation about science; it is an effort to extend the boundaries of knowledge in a science field. By the same token, humanistic research should be more than an investigation of the humanities; it must be research *in* the humanities. The humanities are "the branches of learning concerned with human thought and relations, as distinguished from the sciences." Hence, humanistic research should be concerned with "human thought and relations" as expressed in language, literature, the fine arts, history, and philosophy. This involves more than facts and figures or activities and achievements; it should include human relations, ideas, and ideals. In short, the building blocks of the humanities are *values,* as distinguished from the objective facts and the hypotheses supported by them which are the bricks and mortar of the natural sciences.

The humanities have two basic objectives: the one is disciplinary; the other, a knowledge and understanding of one's heritage. The achievement of each involves the development of values. The disciplinary aim is to develop intellectual interests and initiative and an appreciation of the various methods of communication, such as literature, music, art, and drama. On the other hand, knowledge and appreciation of our past are essential to a humanistic program, as also are the ideas and ideals upon which our culture rests.

Students of the classics become acquainted with the heroic deeds of the past, the nature of society's achievements, excellence in literary expression, in nobility of purpose, and in the ideals that have motivated society. Through philosophy they are brought into contact with the intellectual and moral issues of the past and with the various attempts at resolving them. In the study of foreign languages, both ancient and modern, one develops facility in the use of his own language and acquires new insights into the meaning of words and phrases used by men of various tongues in expressing their thoughts and feelings. Clarification of meaning and the expansion of vocabulary, which accompany language study, result in the ability not merely to discriminate in the use of words but to think more clearly and to express one's thoughts more accurately and effectively. In addition, foreign language study stimulates perception, imagination, and clarity of thought. The study of literary masterpieces develops one's appreciation of the past, one's vision of the future, and the ability to express his own thoughts with greater precision and effectiveness. The history of the race and its achievements excites one's imagination, admiration, and aspiration. In the fine arts one learns to communicate thought and feeling through other media—music, drama, painting, and sculpture. All these values are derived from the teaching of the humanities as disciplinary subjects—but there are other values as well.

One of the greatest needs of the leader is intellectual initiative and independence. In the study of literature, history, and philosophy one achieves skill in handling abstract ideas and fundamental concepts and the ability to view both sides of issues. If the critical approach to learning is employed in the study of the masterpieces in literature, history, and philosophy, a latent ability to think for one's self is aroused and cultivated. There emerges also, along with initiative and independence, a sense of values. The consideration of intellectual, moral, and spiritual issues, as one is guided in his pursuit of truth, develops quite unconsciously a value system which may be a lifetime possession. The perspective provided by literary, historical, and philosophical studies is the frame of reference within which intellectual, moral, and spiritual values are nurtured. They find expression in the ability to appreciate the beautiful, the good, and the true and to discriminate between these qualities and their opposites.

The second basic objective of humanistic studies is to provide an understanding of our heritage, which consists not merely of the conflicts and struggles of the race or of its successes and its failures but particularly of its hopes and aspirations. The humanities, properly taught, reveal the ideas and ideals that have meant most to the culture of which we are a part. They should clarify the ideals that have motivated our predecessors and suggest other motivations that have determined the direction of social change. The story of the development of ideas, ideals, and motivations is more important than that of communities, states, and nations. They represent the meaning of life and not simply the organization of society. They represent the motive power of human progress. They have been responsible, more than all other factors, for our present outlook and purposes. A fusion of ideas, ideals and motivations has formed the basic tenets upon which our culture rests. These are the important achievements of mankind. They are implicit in much of our literature, but no one has undertaken systematically to identify, analyze, and relate them to social, political, economic, and spiritual activities— despite the fact that we have several thousand years of social history at our command. In this age of competing ideologies, proponents of Western culture have been particularly unsuccessful in making explicit the nature and scope of the ideas and ideals that underlie our modes of thought, institutional systems, and collective faith.

It should not be impossible to trace the basic ideas in literature, history, and philosophy and the ideals developing from them in our present complex civilization; yet few of the vast army of research workers in the field of the humanities have devoted attention to them. They would seem to be as necessary to basic humanistic studies as understanding the properties of matter and the nature of magnetic and electrical forces is to the study of physics, or as knowledge of chemical elements and their combinations is to the study of chemistry. Facts about the past have meaning and importance only as they are related to the ideas, ideals, and motivations that have produced them.

Research into the origin, development, and influence of these ideas and ideals would provide an understanding not only of our heritage but of the mainsprings of our society. This approach to liberal education would focus on fundamentals, would eliminate undue proliferation of courses, would insure appropriate subject matter, and would, therefore, make excellent preparation for the teaching of humanistic studies. Our language and literature are replete with the ideas and the ideals that have motivated social progress; foreign language and literature suggest the motivations behind other cultures and provide a more complete understanding of them than would be possible through any other means. The identification of the ideas and the ideals that give power to the classics may not always be easy, but it would in itself be a useful intellectual exercise. The effect of ideas and ideals on the direction of social change would be the concern of the historian. If historical studies adopted such an approach, it would open up vast areas of fruitful research. Accounting for all historical events are human motivations. The history of the American, as of the French, Revolution is important as a record of the struggle to establish certain ideas of government and its relation to peoples. *Liberté, égalité, fraternité* were the key words, the key ideals, in the French upheaval; essentially similar ones motivated the American Revolution. In philosophy one traces the history of human thought and the conceptions of man's relation to the cosmos, to the world of nature, and to his society. The influence of these conceptions on human society becomes the goal of philosophical studies. What more exciting approach to the study of language and literature, history and philosophy, than to seek to understand the underlying ideas and purposes which have inspired the masterpieces of literature and art, produced the events recorded by history, and motivated mankind in the long struggle toward perfection?

It is combinations of ideas that form the substance of the humanities, as the combinations of atoms to produce molecules is the substance of chemistry. The analysis of ideas involved in a poem, an essay, or a story corresponds to the analysis of elements in a compound chemical substance. This approach to the study of humanities would be not only scientific but conducive to both breadth and depth of scholarship. It opens up new fields of research which have as yet been largely untapped.

Such a concept as that of inalienable rights, its origin, its development, and its effect on the philosophy of life, the social institutions, and the motivations of a society would, for example, constitute a fascinating subject of study. For a student of political philosophy, the tracing of this idea in the laws and constitutions of states would provide a rich field for investigation. Such research could lead one not only through the various English-speaking countries but into other lands. To what extent has this concept gained a foothold in such countries as India, China, Japan, the Slavic nations? If it has failed to take root in these cultures, why has it failed? This and numerous other questions involving the relationship of this ideal to those prevailing in other lands would provide many fruitful research problems.

A student of literature might seek evidences of this concept in various types of literary works—poetry, history, fiction, philosophy, etc. A student of history might trace the effects of various ideas of the individual and of his relationship to government in the development of various nations and in their relation to other nations.

The concept of inalienable rights is but one of many political and social ideals whose origins and development might form the basis of research in the graduate schools and of a new content for the liberal arts curriculum. Students of literature, history, and philosophy alike would find fruitful areas of study under each of the concepts investigated. The content of the study would be determined by the discipline of one's interest. The findings of those in the several disciplines would be mutually helpful in understanding the nature and influence of the concepts studied.

Each of the rights in the Bill of Rights has a history. How did it arise? When? Under what circumstances? In what ways has it been incorporated in the laws and customs of the various civilizations, and how has it influenced modern society? The student of literature, of history, of political science, could explore the origin and development of each of these rights as recorded in literature, in history, in political science. The influence of various basic concepts on the direction of social progress would provide an almost unlimited field of study and research. Such investigations would give the student a broad background of understanding of our culture.

Such abstract concepts as justice, integrity, fair play, or moral order in the universe could each be utilized as objects of research by graduate students in a variety of disciplines, such as literature, economics, political science, history, philosophy, and religion.

In the conflict between democracy and totalitarianism, there has been much discussion in recent decades, of the concept of human dignity. When was it crystallized as a working principle? To what extent does it still prevail, and how does one account for those states that have completely denied the concept in both theory and practice. Hitler's plan of extinguishing the Jewish people, and his slaughter of six million members of that people, represents the most outrageous example in history of the violation of this concept, which has played so large a part in the development of the democratic state. How does one account for such a lapse? What are the forces at work in modern society that could turn the clock back for generations?

A single concept, fully studied, beginning with its origins and tracing its development and its influence, citing examples of its neglect and of its application, its varying adaptations, and its influence on human society, would call for a vast amount of research involving history, literature, and philosophy.

Such an approach would give new meaning to facts, provide perspective, assist understanding, and aid articulation between the graduate school and the college. An advantage of this approach is the natural opportunity it affords for the study of other cultures. It might be difficult to understand the basic ideas in Hindu culture, for example, but it is less difficult than undertaking to master its vast literature. One cannot hope to read all the literature, history, and philosophy of all cultures, past and present, but one could master considerable knowledge of the basic ideals and motivations that underlie the major cultures of modern times, together with the evolution of these concepts since many of them are common to all cultures. Such might be considered the equipment of the educated man if our higher education were prepared to provide it. Out of it might emerge certain basic tenets which lie back of all human society, past and present, which might serve as the foundation for a genuine science of society.

This approach in the graduate school would be readily transmitted to the college through the Ph.D.'s who had this new type of training. It would make for articulation between the two divisions of higher education, assist students in the integration of knowledge, reduce the multiplicity of courses, and give new vitality and meaning to the arts college, perhaps in time restoring it to its former position as the central core of higher education.

The paucity of suitable topics for doctor's dissertations is evident to one who examines a published list of abstracts. Moreover, one is impressed with the number of topics that have little or no relation to the subjects that the Ph.D. graduate will be expected to teach. If medical, legal, or engineering training were as far removed from the demands of these professions as the Ph.D. training often is from the subjects to be taught by the college instructor, these professions would be fifty years behind the times.

Thus, there is great need for new areas of investigation in the humanities which would train the candidate for the profession he plans to enter. The lack of articulation between the undergraduate and the graduate programs in American higher education underlies a series of problems in colleges and universities which have plagued educators for years. Among these are the decline of the liberal arts, the difficulty of recruitment for graduate work, the shortage of properly qualified college teachers, the proliferation of courses in the college, and the inability of the colleges to attract many of the ablest young people to teaching.

The basic approach to liberal education which involves an identification of the significant ideas and ideals that constitute the foundation of our culture, would provide a vast array of appropriate topics for master's theses and doctoral dissertations which could transform graduate education in the humanities and at the same time provide the most appropriate education for those planning to teach in a liberal arts college. It would give new meaning and vitality to humanistic studies. It would also provide a new sense of purpose and give the arts college a new status and a new independence.

A major complaint is that the arts college has no longer a basic purpose of its own but is now mainly a service division of the university, providing for the general education needs of professional students. This situation results from the lack of clearly defined goals, which, in turn, derives from the fact that teachers educated in the graduate schools have themselves formed no clear conception of the role of the arts college in the education of youth.

An analysis of *Dissertation Abstracts* (July 1960) will illustrate. Under the humanities twenty-two dissertations dealt with languages and literature, including linguistics, thirteen with speech and theater, nine with history, and five with philosophy. A few examples of the topics will throw further light on the nature of the Ph.D. programs: "A Descriptive Phonology of Standard French," "An Experimental Study of the Effects of Interaural Temporal Delays and Intensity Differences on Intra-Cranial Localization of Spondee Words," "The History of Educational Television—1932-1958," "Differential Thresholds for Frequency in Neuro-Sensory Hearing Loss," "A Theory of the Interpretative Approach to Oral Reading."

Several questions arise in connection with these topics. Speech, theater, and linguistics are ordinarily grouped under the humanistic studies, but they do not conform to the usual conception of the humanities as the core of liberal education. How representative of American higher learning are they? Research on these subjects earned for the students the coveted

Ph.D. There is serious doubt whether some topics are worthy of investigation for any advanced degree, however useful the findings may be to specialists in the fields. But it is even more difficult to think of such researches as representing humane scholarship.

Other questions arise when one considers the profession for which these studies are assumed to be the preparation. A large percentage of Ph.D.'s, in the humanities particularly, become college teachers. Presumably all of those whose dissertations are listed above are now teaching in colleges. In what sense have their researches contributed to their effectiveness as teachers? Doctors of Philosophy, in the humanities especially, are sought after by the liberal arts colleges because of the breadth of their training; and yet most of the topics listed represent a high degree of specialization.

If the focus of attention in the humanities were on the significant ideas and ideals of our culture, a series of significant topics would readily suggest themselves. In Western culture the following concepts are significant but little understood:

Human dignity	Liberty	Fair play
Social justice	Security	Authoritarianism
Integrity	Social responsibility	Totalitarianism
Freedom of speech	Inalienable rights	Fascism
Freedom of assembly	Socialism	Nazism
Freedom of worship	Democracy	Communism

These are but a few examples of concepts that have affected profoundly the course of history.

For the historian, the evolution of each concept or of some facet of it would provide a subject of investigation worthy of an advanced degree. The student of literature, whether English, American, French, or German, could take some idea or combination of ideas and trace their influence on current or past writings. Indeed, literature has frequently exercised great influence on the thought of its time and, hence, may be considered one of the powerful forces in the promotion of ideals and concepts. To take a single example, consider the writings of Tom Paine at the time of the American Revolution and their effect on the colonists in the struggle for independence and in the efforts to establish a new republic. Similarly, the philosopher could deal with these concepts, their philosophical origins, and their influence upon society as a whole. Thus, an abundance of material would be available to challenge the research efforts of all humanistic scholars, whatever their subject of specialization.

Scholars who have had this type of research would be in a position, as teachers, to reshape the arts college curriculum and inject new vitality into this segment of higher education. In this way graduate schools could take the lead, as they properly should, in reviving interest in liberal education.

The research spirit is needed in the arts college as well as in the graduate school. No one can impart the love of learning to youth who does not exhibit it. But for research to be effective in stimulating students, it must somehow be related to the world in which they live. The approach here suggested would have that virtue. Substantive instruction should begin with concepts familiar to students and move on to a study of the meaning and background of the ideals that have motivated our way of life. What more effective approach to liberal education could be suggested?

Such an approach is relevant in our world of conflicting ideologies. The ultimate strength of a nation is the faith of its people in the principles and ideals that dominate their lives. Conviction founded on tradition lacks the power of a faith rooted in knowledge as well as in tradition. This point is incidental to the plan proposed, in its educational aspects, but is of sufficient importance to warrant reference in this connection.

This proposal has other educational implications. One of the problems that have beset the college is the growing body of knowledge and the difficulty of choosing what is essential to the liberally educated person. By discovering the principles and the concepts underlying phenomena, one achieves understanding more readily and with greater economy of time and energy.

Few would disagree with these general statements about the method of giving meaning to history, literature, and philosophy. Yet the great emphasis in college teaching is often upon facts, style of writing, metaphysical concepts, etc., which have little or no relation to humanistic understanding. Likewise, in graduate studies and research, attention is focused on topics about which facts can be readily assembled. Emphasis upon significant ideas and concepts is rarely found among the subjects chosen for research by the student. It appears that no systematic study has been undertaken by graduate faculties or students of the basic elements in our heritage, the significant ideals and concepts, their origin and development and their influence upon human progress.

The burden of this section is to urge that major attention be given to the foundations of our culture in graduate education programs in the humanities. The decline of the *liberal* arts is, by all odds, the most disturbing fact of American higher education. Any basic reforms looking to their rejuvenation must begin in the graduate schools, for they provide the teachers. They have the responsibility of undertaking to restore the arts college to its former central position in higher education.

The welfare of the graduate school itself is dependent upon the vitality of the college, for the latter prepares students for graduate work. If college students have failed to receive sound and vital education, the graduate school will reflect that failure. Professional schools will also be seriously affected by any weakness in liberal education, for they depend upon the college for the basic education of their students. In short, the entire system of higher education has a stake in the quality of the college. Nothing is more obvious than either this or the fact that any fundamental reforms in the college must originate in the graduate school.

CHAPTER 6

Graduate Education

in the Social Sciences

Essentially the same problem of adjusting research and graduate work in the humanities prevails in the social sciences. The method employed in the natural sciences is not well suited to advanced work in the social sciences, which are concerned with *values* just as the humanities are. As in the case of the humanities, the brick and mortar of the social sciences are not facts only but include also ideals, concepts and motivations.

The attempt to apply strictly the natural science method to social studies has been one of the causes of the decline in the vitality of liberal education. Facts are, of course, essential to research of any kind, but they are not the goal of advanced work in sociology, economics, and political science as they are in biology, chemistry, and physics. They are actually means to the end of understanding human values. A synthesis of the discovered facts must take place before a concept of values is achieved. Such a synthesis is not required in the natural sciences, where a single new fact discovered may be sufficient to prove or disprove a hypothesis.

Research in the humanities and social sciences is, therefore, more complex than it is in physics or chemistry. It requires synthesis as well as analysis. Of course, minor aspects of social institutions or organizations can be investigated and results obtained following the method of the natural sciences. For example, one could investigate "The Legal Aspects of Supervising Student Personnel in Selected Secondary Schools" or "The

Relationship between College Academic Performance and Expectancies" just as one could investigate "Action of Oxidizing Agents on Salts of Nitro Compounds," and with equally satisfactory results. While the first two topics were the subjects of dissertations that won for the authors doctor's degrees in social science fields, they could scarcely be thought of as representing basic research in the social sciences. Yet they are fairly representative of current social science topics.

Professors with Ph.D.'s, research for which is no more substantial than that for these topics, would not be prepared to teach the social sciences as liberal arts subjects. Even if *basic* research in the social sciences is more difficult than that required of most graduate students, this is not an adequate reason for failure to attempt it. Such research is especially needed in these times when the tenets of Western culture are being attacked.

The new approach so badly needed is not likely to be developed unless the graduate schools take the initiative. The faculties are responsible for the type of research conducted by graduate students. This, in turn, affects the tone and emphasis in college instruction. Surely both research and instruction should reflect concern for fuller understanding of the issues of our time and of what is happening in the world. This is the traditional role of universities. As Ortega y Gasset, in his *Mission of the University,* said, ". . . it is imperative to set up once more, in the university, the teaching of culture, the system of vital ideas, which the age has attained. This is the basic function of the university. This is what the university must be, above all else."[1]

This aspect of the university's responsibility will be considered further later in this chapter. Let us now turn to a more detailed consideration of the social sciences, the nature of their limitations and of their relation to the natural sciences.

Little progress was made in the natural sciences before the elements of each were defined and analyzed. For example, in

---

[1] José Ortega y Gasset, *Mission of the University,* trans. H. L. Nostrand (Princeton: Princeton University Press, 1944), p. 59.

physics, standard measures of weight, time, mass, length and volume had to be defined and agreed upon before they could be used as tools of investigation. When the theory of gravity evolved the strength of the earth's magnetic field had to be determined; and when electricity was discovered, the force of an electric current had to be measured (volts and amperes). Likewise, heat and cold, light and darkness, and the properties and nature of gases, liquids, and solids had to be defined.

In chemistry the concern is with the composition of all matter and with the changes that take place in it under given conditions. It deals with inorganic, organic, and physical matter. The atom, its combination with other atoms to form molecules, and the elements found in nature are the foundation of the science of chemistry.

In biology, life in plants and in animals, including the human animal, is the object of study. It includes the processes of growth and decay as well as the classification of species.

On the other hand, the objects with which the humanistic-social sciences deal are ideas, ideals, and motivations, together with the institutions that have developed from them. Their origin, development, and influence in human society, on the analogy of the natural sciences, should be the foundation of the various humanistic studies. In the case of the social sciences there is more concern with the institutions that have crystallized around ideals and concepts. For example, economics deals with the conditions and laws affecting the production, distribution, and consumption of wealth for the material means of satisfying human desires; political science, with the organization and government of communities, states, and nations; sociology, with the elements, processes, and consequences of group living; and ethics, with moral duty and the principles of conduct.

There are certain ideas that underlie all of the social sciences. There are others of special relevance to each of them. For example, freedom, equality, rights, duties, responsibilities, are common alike to sociology, economics, and political science. Free public schools and hospital service, free enterprise in business and industry, and free election on the local, state, and national levels derive from the same notion of man's relation to his society. Similarly, if such basic concepts as honesty, integrity, and justice and the institutions that society has designed to foster them are being considered, they need not be taught under three headings—economics, sociology, and political science—for they apply alike to all three. In addition to these elements common to all the social sciences, concepts of special relevance to each might be illustrated by the following. In economics, competition, fair play, money, credit, banking, property, etc., are the elements involved. Political science, on the other hand, is concerned with the franchise, justice, law, restraints, controls—both legal and political—and the political systems under which society has developed. The elements that concern sociology are processes, purposes, and consequences of group living and the institutions that have developed from certain basic ideas.

Since no science of society has been formulated, the social sciences are still in the stage of clarifying the basic elements in social organizations, institutions and controls and interaction of these several ideas and ideals upon each other. No one has undertaken to establish axioms, postulates, and hypotheses upon which a science of society might rest as securely as chemistry and physics rest upon their axioms, postulates, and the facts established by investigation.

Until it identifies the elements with which it deals, social science is in the position of the science of chemistry before the various chemical elements and the molecular structure of matter were recognized.

If the emphasis in the social sciences were upon the ideas and ideals that have given rise to social, economic, and political institutions, rather than merely upon the institutions themselves, there would be a more fundamental understanding of their character. This approach opens up vast new areas of fruitful investigation. It is the great challenge to the social scientist whatever his field of interest. Such an approach must first be made by the graduate schools where the prospective teacher is being prepared.

Perhaps a single example will suffice to ilustrate. Education is the most universal of secular institutions. As early as the third century b.c., Plato's *Republic* outlined a system of education based on certain ideas and ideals of society that he conceived to be valid. In the Roman period Quintilian, in his *Institutes of Oratory,* set forth a plan for the education of youth which reflected the thoughts and ideals of his time. Pestalozzi, Froebel, Montessori, and a host of others presented new purposes and new methods as guides to the education of youth. In England charitable organizations, as early as the eighteenth century, took an interest in giving the children of the poor the chance for a more abundant life. This approach was prompted by religious motivation, but it was followed by a more general interest and state support, as the king recognized the advantages to the state of educated subjects. Education found its full expression in the democratic state, which emphasizes it as essential to stability and progress. Thus, a wide variety of ideas, ideals, and motivations has given rise to public and private education at the lower levels. To identify these and trace their influence on education, as we know it today, would constitute a fascinating and rewarding study. University education, based largely on a different set of ideals and concepts, is another facet of the broad subject of education. Dating back to the twelfth century in Western culture, it provides a fruitful field of study and research.

In a similar manner, the ideals and concepts of government developed from tribal to feudal, to unlimited and limited monarchy, to oligarchy, and finally to democracy. Democratic forms could be identified and traced through the evolution of social organization and controls. In economics the motivations responsible for the development of money, credit, and banking and the conceptions of ownership, of free enterprise, of the corporation, and of the production, distribution, and consumption of wealth could be identified in the structure and activities of economic institutions.

Such a fundamental approach in the study of the social sciences would provide not merely knowledge of social organizations and institutions but an understanding of their backgrounds and influence. It would provide not only social understanding but perspective and the basis for value judgments. One of the unresolved issues in social science and humanities instruction is the means of inculcating a sense of values. With an understanding of the ideals and motivations of the past, it should be possible to make clear which value system most nearly conforms to our traditions and goals.

One of the significant debates in modern higher education concerns whether it is possible, within the framework of objective instruction, to do more than describe different value systems, leaving the student to make his choice.

The orthodox position of social scientists has been stated by one of them as follows: "Scientific method, as such, provides no techniques for answering questions of value, for determining ultimate ends, for weighing the merits of an ethical and political controversy, for deciding what, if anything, ought to be done as a matter of social policy." On the other hand, a prominent economist argues persuasively that:

The orthodox position is essentially false, that it rests upon an unwarranted and outmoded dichotomy between means and ends, between facts and values; that it confuses issues which concern the achievements of science with the issues pertaining to scientific methodology; and that it is inconsistent with newer developments in epistemology and metaphysics.

Graduate school leadership is needed in the effort to resolve so fundamental an issue. The introduction of the new approach in social science research and graduate instruction might point the way. The concentration of research on the ideals and concepts that underlie social institutions not only should assist in clarifying the goals of social science instruction but should give substance to the various social science disciplines.

Such an approach in social science instruction and research should give the student a fullness of view, a pattern of thinking, a set of standards by which he may be guided in the choice of alternatives. This is not adequately provided in the present curriculum. Fragments of knowledge, gleaned from the study of a series of subjects, treated as isolated specialities, do not meet the need. A comprehensive analysis of the underlying ideals and concepts of our society should provide a framework within which the factual subject matter of social science would have a deeper meaning.

This would provide a common background for the study of the several social science subjects and, thus, would aid in the integration of subject matter. By the same token, it would contribute to a fuller understanding of the issues involved when conflict arises.

The present situation in the world emphasizes the need for this approach. The United States has a longer experience with democracy than any other country. Other lands look to us for guidance. The "revolution of rising expectations" highlights this fact. Men everywhere are clamoring for the right to self-government—for example, the new nations arising in Africa. *The Rockefeller Panel Report on American Democracy* sums up the matter eloquently:

> Men everywhere are living through a change of the human scene that challenges most ideas and institutions inherited from other days. Man's relation to his physical environment has changed; his relation to other men, his distance from them, and impact upon them have changed; his sense of himself and of the possibilities of human life have changed. And behind these changes there are momentous and irreversible movements that have brought a tidal shift in the course of human affairs.[2]

In the midst of such a revolutionary period the United States has its greatest challenge and opportunity. It is a sad commentary on the state of the social sciences for social scientists to be arguing that they may explain different value systems but cannot, within the framework of objective scholarship, suggest which is preferable; it is not only unrealistic but tragic in the light of what is happening in the world around us.

[2] *The Rockefeller Panel Report on American Democracy* (New York: Doubleday & Co., 1960), p. 61.

Fundamental research in the social sciences requires focusing attention on the significant ideas and ideals that underlie our culture; their identification should be followed by a study of their origins, growth, and influence on American society. This approach to the problem of understanding our value system is both scientific and relevant to this ideological age. With such a body of knowledge of the foundations of our culture, the basis is laid for saying what is true or false in the light of history. Not only are American youth in need of such dynamic instruction but the youthful nations of the world, which are groping for the light, are seeking just such guidance.

The great changes that have occurred since World War II have apparently had little or no effect on the program of graduate instruction in our universities and scarcely more on the curriculum of the college. Since basic changes in instructional content and methods in the colleges wait upon changes in the graduate school, this problem should be given a high priority in graduate education. A recasting of social science content and method is a reform seriously needed in American higher education. If one doubts this, it is suggested that he take a look at a list of dissertation topics and abstracts. On an examination of several such lists the author failed to find a single dissertation that dealt with really significant problems. It might be argued that the Ph.D. candidate is not mature enough to be expected to make a contribution toward the solution of basic problems, that he should be encouraged to choose a manageable topic. But there are surely facets of significant issues which would be appropriate for a dissertation. Significant ideas and concepts have histories, the tracing of which would provide projects for research that could be both exacting and exciting. Instead, one finds subjects like "Social Status and Masculinity-Feminity," "A Study of the Professional Role of a Dentist", and "Structures and Orientations of Retail Business: A Typological Study."

These examples are cited not as a criticism but as a comment on the kind of research that is sponsored by American graduate education and for which the highest degree, the Ph.D., is awarded. Does such research represent American higher learning or what it ought to be? What about the value of such investigation as preparation for college teaching? Is it the kind of research that is designed to advance the cause of liberal education?

Mr. McGrath suggested that the graduate schools were responsible for the decline of the liberal arts. He maintains that "during the expansion of graduate education the liberal arts began to surrender their independence: Gradually they relinquished the function which for centuries in British, and later in American, higher education had been their heritage and their glory, to wit, the function of instructing young people in the Western European intellectual and spiritual tradition."[3] While this statement cannot be denied, the reasons why this has happened are not so clear.

Is it because graduate education and research unfit one for teaching in a college? I think not. Indeed, I believe that the best teacher is usually the one who is pursuing active research and study. The effectiveness of research as preparation for college teaching depends upon the kind of research pursued.

It is the *type* of research that affects adversely the arts college and tends to defeat the purposes of liberal education. This suggests that the orientation of research in the humanities and the social sciences may be the source of the difficulty. If significant ideals and concepts became the focus in the humanities, and if the institutions that have sprung from them became the center of attention in the social sciences, there would seem to be no reason why the graduate school experience should not fit the Ph.D. for teaching in the arts college and thereby serve to advance the cause of liberal education rather than retard it.

There are also other untapped areas that should attract the interest of social scientists and would be appropriate and relevant in these times. For example, the problem our society has of adjusting to changes that are imposed by an advancing science

[3] Earl J. McGrath, *The Graduate School and the Decline of Liberal Education,* Bureau of Publications, Teachers College, Columbia, p. 14.

and technology is one of great magnitude. These changes affect our daily lives in the home, in the community, in the state, and in the nation. They have much to do with "the revolution of rising expectations" of men and women around the world. The research programs in the universities, in the graduate schools, and among graduate students reflect no concern over this problem.

A basic reason for including the social sciences in the arts college curriculum is the need for helping youth to understand their society, something of the currents and countercurrents operative in it, its complexity, its history, and the factors affecting its stability and progress.

What a mine of appropriate and relevant topics for M.A. theses and doctoral dissertations would be available if the proper orientation were provided in the graduate school. What has been the effect on our society of railroads, the telephone and telegraph, the automobile, radio, television, the airplane, etc., etc.? What have the effects been of the discovery of atomic fission at the local, state, national, and international levels?

The sociologist, the economist, and the political scientist, all would have an abundance of topics worthy of investigation. Moreover, the results of the findings would be useful in many different ways. More would be required than the application of the slide rule or the computer. Considerable cerebration would be essential for effective research in these areas, for one would have to consider many facets of each problem and many factors that are not always easily discernible. More thinking and less mere accumulation of facts is, after all, the great need in graduate education, in theses and dissertations, and in other graduate school research.

The type of research here suggested requires not only an analytical process, which is involved in the search for facts, but also the ability to synthesize, in order to determine the over-all impact of a series of influences on the family, on the community, or on society as a whole. Much of the research engaged in at the graduate student level is concerned chiefly with analysis, with facts, and involves a minimum of synthesis or of intellectual judgment.

One of the major objectives of liberal education is the development of attitudes, ideals, a sense of values, and the ability to reach sound conclusions based on evidence. One who has achieved this objective develops a set of convictions and a reasoned philosophy of life, on the basis of which his activities are guided. Such an outlook serves to give balance to his thoughts and actions and stability to his purposes and strivings. These qualities are at a premium today. They are essential to sanity and to effectiveness. Much of the frustration, unhappiness, and inefficiency of our times derives from the lack of these qualities, which characterize the liberally educated. A man without convictions is like a rudderless ship that is subject to the buffetings of the wind and the waves. As Socrates suggested more than two thousand years ago, "If a man does not know to what port he is sailing, no wind is favorable."

Research and study of the foundations of our culture and of the institutions that have stemmed from them, are basic to liberal education. If, added to this, provision is made for a study of the factors constantly forcing changes in the social structure, such as those resulting from an advancing science and technology, the foundations would be laid for a vital social science program which would have much to contribute to liberal education.

This is but another way of suggesting that it is not *research* itself but the *kind* of research engaging the attention of graduate students, who became teachers in the humanistic-social studies field, that has affected adversely the colleges of arts and sciences. This is at variance, in some respects, with the view expressed by Mr. McGrath when, in speaking of the "current disordered educational scheme," he said:

It is clear—that in order to restore liberal education to the central position it once rightly occupied in American higher education, the institutions which should provide that education must reaffirm their high purposes and pursue them with renewed dedication. This they cannot do until they are freed from the restrictions imposed by other much younger, but organizationally stronger, units in the American system of higher education, namely, the graduate schools, which continue to be animated by the spirit of the German university.[4]

The preparation of prospective teachers provided by the graduate school in recent decades is doubtless responsible for the present plight of the college, because the type of research fostered by the graduate schools has been at cross purposes with the arts college. But it need not be so. I am, therefore, in full agreement with the statement that "only drastic reforms in graduate education will permit a much-needed reorientation of liberal education" and that "before any substantial reconstruction can occur —the purposes of graduate education must be revised and clarified."[5]

In the humanities and the social sciences the strict application of methods employed in natural science research often results in dissertation topics that are unsuited to those preparing for teaching in liberal arts colleges. Clearly, reforms in the subject matter of research and in the methods of graduate instruction are necessary before articulation between the undergraduate and graduate programs can be achieved. This is a central issue in graduate education and must be resolved before integration in higher education can take place.

Mr. McGrath refers to the graduate school as "organizationally stronger" than the arts college. But a close examination of the relationship reveals that the graduate school, as an organization, is without power. Its influence over the college has been exercised through its preparation of college teachers. Actually the college faculty in most universities can veto almost any change proposed by the graduate faculty. One department, even, can turn down the recommendations of the graduate council. Precedent for this dates back to 1890, when the Harvard faculty voted that the graduate department and the Lawrence Scientific School should be under the control of the faculty of arts.

[4] *Ibid.*, p. 13.
[5] *Ibid.*, p. 25.

Though in most universities the faculty of arts still has authority over the graduate faculty, it does not control what is taught in the graduate school or how it is taught. It is the teaching and the research of the graduate faculty, in the preparation of college teachers, that have affected the college. Thus, while the graduate school is *organizationally* subordinate to the college, the college is *educationally* dominated by the graduate school. This paradoxical relationship between the undergraduate and the graduate divisions of higher education accounts for much of the confusion that emerges in discussions involving their interrelations.

To summarize the findings of this section of the report on graduate education in the social sciences, it may effect economy of time and effort if the chief points are itemized with comments on each for the purpose of clarification:

1. Social studies, as now taught, are not sciences in the sense that chemistry, physics, or biology are. In neither the humanities nor the social studies is there a body of basic knowledge, built up by patient research, which could serve as a foundation for a superstructure such as is found in the natural sciences. Despite this basic difference between the humanistic-social studies and the natural sciences, the pattern of research in both areas has been the same. The outcomes have, therefore, been different. The unsatisfactory results in humanities and social studies research stem from this fact. Significant ideas and ideals constitute the warp and woof of the humanistic-social studies fields. But these have not been identified, much less systematically organized to serve as a foundation for further investigation. Hence, a major concern of graduate and research work in non-scientific fields should be to identify the fundamental tenets which underlie our culture and which find expression in our social institutions.

2. After these basic elements in our social structure have been identified and their origin and development traced, research into the nature of their influence on social institutions and social progress would be a logical next step. Such research, pursued

over a long period, might produce the foundations upon which a true science of society could be constructed. This should be the ultimate goal of humanistic-social studies.

3. In both these areas education in *values* is fundamental. They are indispensable to effective instruction and research. Here again is a matter that has special relevance for non-science fields. Values may be derived and identified from a study of the basic ideals, motivations, and convictions of our society. Such an approach moves in the direction of converting the social studies into "social sciences." But before the process can be completed, much patient and painstaking investigation and research will be required.

4. This approach in the humanities and social studies involves reorientation of the graduate education curriculum, a different emphasis in research for the master's and doctor's degrees, and a different type of thesis and dissertation. To achieve this will require special research and planning, if satisfactory results are to be expected.

5. Another broad area of study, which should engage the attention of faculties and graduate students in the social science field, is that of effective adjustment to the social changes imposed by an advancing science and technology. The incredible scientific and technological progress of recent years highlights the need for such an emphasis, and the prospects of still more rapid advances before the end of this century suggest its central importance.

So great is the need for a new and imaginative approach to more effective instruction in the humanistic-social studies area, and so enormous is the amount of research required to develop that approach, that a decade may be necessary to complete the task. It should be a joint undertaking of the college and the graduate school, with some help also from the professional schools. They, like the graduate school, are dependent upon the college for the basic training of their students. The graduate school has the major responsibility for this program, since it must begin there before it can reach the college.

CHAPTER 7

*Graduate Education
and the Liberal Arts*

Students of higher education agree that the plight of liberal education in the United States is disturbing, but they are not unanimous with respect to the cause or how it has happened. As already noted, McGrath suggests that the graduate schools must be held accountable for the situation, citing the fact that the decline in the role of the arts college has paralleled the rise of graduate education. He submits some evidence that there is a causal relation, that the emphasis on specialized research and graduate work has resulted in the loss of prestige and effectiveness of the arts college.

But to accept this as a fact still does not explain how it has happened. Is it because graduate professors have disparaged liberal education in their zeal for scientific research, or is it that specialized investigation and the liberal arts are antithetical and will not mix? Is it the kind of research—specialized objective and dehumanized—that is at fault? Could it be that the expansion of knowledge, for which the graduate schools are largely responsible, has resulted in a flooding of the college curriculum, thereby producing confusion and the loss of a sense of direction in the college? Is it possible that graduate professors in the humanities and social sciences have not recognized clearly the difference between the type of research required in history, language, literature, and philosophy and that which is effective in biology, chemistry, physics, and geology?

These are all questions that warrant detailed consideration.

In seeking the answers, it may be possible to clarify some aspects of the problem that have been confused and to discover some factors that have been overlooked in previous discussions.

The query about the attitude of graduate professors toward liberal education is easily answered. With few exceptions, members of the graduate school faculties are the most ardent advocates of basic education. As Mr. McGrath found in his study of the attitudes of graduate and professional faculty members, the need for more and better liberal education is almost universally recognized. Not only medical and law, but engineering and agricultural professors were equally strong in their belief in the liberal arts.

The question relating to the compatibility of specialized research and arts college instruction is more difficult to answer. The college professor who is enamored with "knowing more and more about less and less," who is engaged in his free time with specialized research, is not likely to find the atmosphere of the college classroom congenial. His role as a teacher might be handicapped by his research interest. He can justify considering teaching secondary to research, since the administration generally rewards publication with promotion and salary increase, whereas good teaching is often not so recognized. In such a case institutional policy and specialized interests are both at fault.

There is, however, another side to the coin. The enthusiasm of the genuine scholar is contagious. A teacher with a real research interest, who also enjoys teaching—and there are many such professors—often kindles the fires of intellectual curiosity among the more gifted students which would be left smoldering by a *good* teacher whose intellectual interests had died down. Nothing can spark the intellectual tinder in young, alert minds like excitement over discovery of new knowledge on the part of the instructor. An intellectually active mind is the first requisite of the really great teacher. Long experience with college faculties suggests that much more poor teaching results from a lack of research interest than from an excess of it.

A third aspect of the relationship between specialized scholarship and the arts college is the nature of the problems investigated in the graduate schools. The professor of Greek who did his dissertation on the "Genitive Case of the Parts of the Body in Greek Tragedy," or the professor of sociology who did his research magnum opus on "Social Status and Masculinity-Femininity" or the economics professor who produced a dissertation on "The Distribution of Empty Freight Cars," would probably not be better professors of Greek, sociology, or economics because of their research efforts. They might even be unfitted rather than helped by their graduate school activities, but that would not be because they had engaged in research, but because of the type of research pursued. In such cases the graduate school cannot escape responsibility for the result.

Insofar as graduate schools have been responsible for the explosion of knowledge in the past few decades, they may be considered indirectly accountable for one of the difficulties experienced by the colleges in recent years, but no one would consider this a *fault* of graduate education. It is not, however, unreasonable to suggest that the leaders of graduate education might have helped solve the problem of proliferation of courses in the colleges if they had been alert to it and had modified the program of teacher preparation in the graduate schools in such way as to have avoided unwarranted additions to the curriculum.

The relation of the curriculum to the increase in knowledge is illustrated by a brief sketch of its growth. For example, philosophy was originally the core of the college, along with Latin, Greek, and Hebrew. This was subdivided into *moral* philosophy and *natural* philosophy. The former spawned the social sciences —ethics, sociology, economics, and political science. Natural philosophy was the forerunner of the natural sciences—chemistry, physics, biology, and geology. These were the basic subjects for decades, and then further subdivisions occurred—biochemistry, biophysics, microbiology, bacteriology, geophysics, physical chemistry. The social sciences expanded to include anthropology, psychology (now sometimes listed under the natural sciences), educational psychology, child psychology, social psychology, physiological psychology. Then sociology was divided into principles of sociology, rural sociology, urban sociology, and so on ad infinitum.

This listing of college offerings could be multiplied tenfold and still not include all catalogue announcements. In the midst of such a plethora of courses what can the colleges do? As Mr. McGrath pointed out, twenty-five to thirty different courses are listed under *liberal education*. This fragmentation of knowledge has occurred without anyone planning it. Each year has seen new courses added and usually none subtracted. Multiplication of courses has been deplored for years, but no solution has been proposed. As a result the process goes on apace. As new knowledge is discovered, new courses are added.

It has long been recognized that selection of subject matter is necessary. The general education movement, a massive effort to meet that need, represents an attempt to identify the elements of knowledge essential to the liberally educated person and to combine these in a single curriculum. While this approach has been useful, it has lacked one important ingredient: it provides no criteria by which to distinguish between essential and nonessential subject matter.

A curriculum organized around the significant ideals and concepts of our culture, as suggested in the two preceding chapters, would provide such a criterion. In the first place, these are the basis of our culture. Facts, events, and activities are the results of the ideals that have given direction and stability to social progress. They have inspired the great literature and the significant events in our history and provided the philosophical, moral, and spiritual foundations of our culture. They underlie the goals and methods of our society, our social institutions, and our way of life.

The accumulation of knowledge is so great that it is impossible to acquire any major fraction of it in a lifetime, much less in four college years. Consequently some basis for selecting subject matter for the college curriculum is imperative. If significant ideals, concepts, and goals in our society were chosen as focuses, the curriculum not only would contain the essentials of liberal education but would require fewer departments, fewer courses, and perhaps fewer teachers.

The emphasis of such a program suggests other benefits. Among college faculties and administrative officers there is great interest in the problem of inculcating *values*. It is recognized that one's sense of values is the most important element in his personality. However brilliant intellectually one may be, his usefulness to society is reckoned in terms of the *values* by which he is guided. A highly trained brilliant mind may produce society's number one benefactor or its number one enemy. The scale of values by which he is motivated makes the difference. Hence, educators and laymen alike must be concerned about how education can assist the student in the formulation and cultivation of a sound sense of values. The present arts college program makes little provision for this phase of education.

The plan proposed here for the humanities and the social sciences provides for the cultivation of values. In identifying the significant ideals and concepts, all the judgments concern values. In the tracing of their history and influence on society, value judgments would be constantly required. Undergraduate instruction under the plan would contribute directly and significantly to the development of a sense of values. Likewise, in graduate and research work the thesis or dissertation would require basic investigation involving value judgments. For example, a dissertation on some aspect of man's inalienable rights would involve consideration of the importance of each idea contributing to the concept and of the nature and importance of the influence the concept has had on the social, economic, and political life of the United States.

Students of literature might search out the poems, essays, or fiction that were inspired by this conception of man's relation to his universe. Both religious and secular literature would need to be covered in the search for the origin and development of this and other related ideas and concepts. The historian and the political scientist might search for the origin and examples of this concept in historical tradition or in political history. This kind of research would not, like statistical and factual studies, consist chiefly in arraying a series of facts to prove or disprove some hypothesis, but would require a critical appraisal of the motivations behind the concept of inalienable rights, a synthesis of these findings, and an understanding of the social theory from which such a concept emerged.

Obviously research on such a topic would be admirable preparation for teaching in a liberal arts college. The Ph.D., fresh from graduate study, would have not only much information to give students on a fundamental subject but an attitude toward basic issues in our society that would permeate his instruction. This should give vitality to teaching and, at the same time, serve as a means of developing a sense of values in those taught.

Two basic complaints against the arts college are: its lack of a sense of direction, which accounts for its failure to evoke the interest of the student; and its failure to assist him in developing a sense of values and a philosophy of life. Such an approach as that suggested should provide both these missing elements because it deals with fundamental ideas and ideals of our society. Surely it is the function of basic education to emphasize those concepts that are the foundation stones of our culture; otherwise, they may in time be forgotten and allowed to disintegrate.

The fear that instruction may lack objectivity and deteriorate into propaganda has had a profound effect on American education. While it is a healthy concern, it can be carried too far. The notion that in social science teaching one may explain different value systems but may not express a preference for one over the other is a case in point. This point of view has affected instruction in both the humanities and the social sciences and may have been in part responsible for their lack of emphasis upon basic issues and concepts. If so, it is of first importance that it be re-examined.

Our colleges have undoubtedly failed to provide an adequate understanding of the ideals that underlie our way of life. If they

fail to impart such understanding, what other agency is there
to perform this function? What more important task could
engage the attention of the colleges and, by the same token, the
graduate schools that prepare college teachers?

The quality of our culture is determined by the ideals that
have dominated it. If higher education fails to make clear the
meaning of those ideals and their influence on our culture,
society suffers. This point is emphasized by John W. Gardner
in his provocative book *Excellence,* in which he says: "The
virtues which flower in any society are the virtues that the
society nourishes. The qualities of mind and character which
stamp a people are the qualities which that people honor, the
qualities they celebrate, the qualities they recognize instantly
and respect profoundly."[1] Liberal education has no greater responsibility than to make clear to youth the qualities of mind
and character that we as a people honor, celebrate, recognize,
and respect. This can be achieved through acquainting them
with the significant ideas and aspirations that inhere in our
history and traditions.

The type of research in the humanistic-social studies field,
which is here proposed, should make liberal education more
attractive and go a long way toward revitalizing the program
of the arts college. It should also provide a natural means of
articulating the work of the graduate and undergraduate divisions, particularly in the humanities and social sciences.

This still leaves the problem of the adjustment of the natural
science graduate instruction to that of the college, an area that
has attracted much attention in recent years.

The effort of Dr. James B. Conant, while president of Harvard
University, to devise a method of teaching science to non-science
majors emphasized a need that had long been neglected and
focused attention on the importance of a new approach in
teaching science as a liberal arts subject. This, in turn, posed
the question of how in the graduate school the prospective

[1] John W. Gardner, *Excellence,* (New York: Harper & Brothers, 1961), p. 151.

teacher could best be prepared to make science teaching contribute to liberal education.

The plan, common in most four-year colleges, of allowing the first year in a natural science to satisfy the science requirement for non-science majors makes little sense. Nevertheless, most colleges still follow the plan for the simple reason that most M.A. and Ph.D. graduates know no way of teaching science other than the one they were taught. The graduate school has not taken seriously its responsibility in this area. It has usually not given its students an understanding of the need for the new approach required in teaching science as a humane subject.

Complaint has frequently been raised against the graduate school for its failure to require professional education courses of those who plan to teach. This may have some merit, but it is of far greater importance that the graduate school faculty require the *kind* of research needed to produce the *kind* of scholar needed for teaching in the arts college. This applies to all three basic divisions of the college. In the two preceding chapters the research needed to produce good teachers in the humanities and in the social sciences has been discussed. It remains here to suggest an approach that might produce good teachers of the natural sciences.

First of all, research in the natural science studied must be pursued, whether it be biology, chemistry, geology, or physics, for one who has not had some experience as a scientist is not prepared to teach science in college. But this should be only one phase of the research required. The other should include either some aspect of the history of science, or an investigation of the influence of science and the scientific method on modern society, or some facet of the philosophy of science.

The obvious objection will be raised that more than three or four years will be required if the Ph.D. candidate must produce two dissertations. As a matter of fact, most candidates for the Ph.D. have already taken a master's degree, for which they had to produce a thesis. The topic for this thesis might be in one of the three fields listed: the history of science (or of a particular science), the influence of science (or of a particular science), or the philosophy of science. Let us examine briefly biology and chemistry with a view to suggesting how research into their backgrounds could be conducted.

Biology, for instance, predates the Christian Era. Alcmaeon, living about 500 B.C., described the optic nerve and the eustachian tubes and began a study of the development of the embryo. A number of the biological works of Aristotle (fourth century B.C.) survive: those dealing with the psyche (*de anima*), history of animals (*historia animalium*), about the generation of animals (*de generatione animalium*), and the parts of animals (*de partibus animalium*). His pupil, Theophrastus, left behind "the most complete biological treatises that have come to us from antiquity."[2] Galen, in the second century A.D., developed an elaborate scheme of physiology which was followed until modern times. These and other early pioneers and the aspects of biology that had their beginnings in these early times, would constitute excellent subjects of study and research for historically minded students.

In the Middle Ages and in the Renaissance numerous students of biology left their "footprints in the sands of time"—such as Albertus Magnus, Leonardo da Vinci, Fabricius, William Harvey, Galileo, each of whom laid the foundations for work in modern biology. In a later period Cuvier, Lamarck, Linnaeus, Darwin, and a host of other life scientists made contributions to modern biology, which are all too often forgotten by contemporary scientists who are engrossed in new discoveries.

To trace the growth of the ideas that any one of the great scientists left behind as his contribution to the world's storehouse of knowledge, and the effect these ideas have had on modern biological science, would constitute a worthy thesis topic and a fascinating study. Nothing could be more valuable in the first year of graduate study for the scientist who will spend his life in the laboratory, and nothing could contribute more to the

[2] *Encyclopedia Britannica.*

effectiveness of the future college or high school teacher of science.

The approach suggested in biology is equally applicable to all other sciences. The origin of chemistry as a science was in Egypt, many centuries before the Christian Era. Alchemy, the forerunner of chemistry, was used in work with metals, glass, and pottery and in tanning and dyeing. Both the Orientals and the Greeks speculated on the nature of the physical world. Thales (640-546 B.C.), a Greek philosopher, considered water the prime element; Anaximenes considered everything sprang from air; Zoroaster (sixth or seventh century B.C.) taught that fire was the symbol of goodness in creation, and among the Greeks, Heraclitus espoused the same theory, while Pherecydes advocated the notion that the earth was the primordial element.

From these beginnings the science of chemistry evolved. So complex is its history and so rapid has been its growth as a science in modern times that one need not go farther back than the seventeenth century in an effort to understand modern chemistry. The names of Boyle, Scheele, Priestley, Lavoisier, Cavendish, Maxwell, Dalton, and Berthollet are but a few of these who stand out as landmarks in the history of modern chemistry. Each was responsible for particular advances. Every chemist working in his laboratory owes a debt of gratitude to them, for they laid the foundation upon which modern chemistry was built.

Any chemistry student with a modicum of intellectual curiosity should find inspiration in a study of how each of these scientists contributed to his field. A part of the program for chemistry majors in the upper two years of college and the first year of graduate work could be an investigation into the background of chemistry through a study of the contributions of one or more of these pioneer chemists. For the non-chemistry majors who take chemistry to fulfill the science requirements, essays on the life and works of its founders could be required in addition to the lectures and laboratory work. In this way the understanding of modern science in general and of chemistry in particular could be greatly enhanced.

Similar programs in physics and geology as well as in biology and chemistry would go far toward humanizing the study of science in the arts and science colleges. This will not occur unless the graduate schools comprehend the need and provide for instruction in the backgrounds of modern science.

This approach in the natural sciences parallels that proposed for the humanities and the social sciences. By studying the origin and development of the seminal concepts in the several sciences and their influence on scientific progress, one acquires a sense of the role of science in modern society. Insofar as it does result in achieving this objective, science can be considered a humane subject, and insofar as the graduate school prepares for teaching science in this way, it is contributing to the advancement of liberal education.

The plan developed by President Conant at Harvard of giving non-science majors an understanding of the meaning of science by acquainting them with the way scientists have made discoveries, is closely related to the plan here proposed. The two plans would be complementary. A study of the concepts developed by pioneering scientists, coupled with the way in which they have undertaken to prove or disprove their hypotheses, would produce graduates who are acquainted not only with science and its role in modern society but with the scientific method as well. This is precisely what liberal education seeks to accomplish.

The practical problem of finding time in the curriculum for this extra work in science is obvious. It might be provided for by an hour's credit for independent study, the writing of papers, and occasional lectures designed to serve as guides to independent study, or the laboratory work could be telescoped for non-science majors, who could use the time thus saved to delve into the background of the science studied. A third of the first year in any science could be profitably used by the humanistic-social studies majors in seeking to understand, through lectures and reading, the meaning of science, something of the structure of the sciences, and their importance in the modern world.

These changes in the curriculum would involve much extra work on the part of faculties in developing reading lists and in recasting the lectures for first-year students. After three to five years, however, the time required of faculties would probably be no greater than it is now. If graduate schools should undertake to prepare their M.S. and Ph.D. graduates, particularly those who plan to teach, to conduct courses on the backgrounds of science and scientists, the new teachers would fit easily into the new program.

If it be true, as Mr. McGrath suggests, that the rise of graduate education has been responsible for the decline of liberal education, the suggested reforms in the graduate schools might be the means of restoring liberal education to its rightful place as the center of university education.

An institution that focuses its chief attention on science, technology, and professional education may have its right to be called a university questioned; it might be more appropriately styled a scientific, technological, or professional institute. The distinguishing characteristic of the university is its emphasis upon basic studies as the foundation for technological and professional curriculums.

The graduate school has the responsibility for initiating whatever changes may be required for the preparation of effective teachers. In other words, in the last analysis the graduate school must be held accountable for lack of articulation between graduate and undergraduate education and for taking such steps as may be necessary to remedy the situation. The faculties of the colleges must also participate in the effort, but they are powerless to effect reforms in liberal education if the graduate education program remains unchanged.

In the past forty years the colleges have instituted a variety of changes—such as honors curriculums, survey courses, interdepartmental programs, and the general education movement—but these have usually been short-lived, partly because the programs of the graduate schools have remained unchanged. On the other hand, as long as the graduate faculty has no authority to effect changes without the approval of all the departments of the college, no significant reforms can be instituted.

Mr. McGrath suggests that the colleges must be freed from the "restrictions imposed by graduate schools" if liberal education is to be restored "to the central position it once rightly occupied in American higher education."[3] The use of the phrase "restrictions imposed by graduate schools" is puzzling. They have no authority to impose restrictions on the colleges. Through their departments the colleges can reject changes proposed by the graduate faculties. However, the colleges cannot escape dependence upon the graduate schools, since the latter prepare the teaching personnel for the former. It is not freedom from the graduate schools but closer cooperation with them in developing an approach to liberal education that is necessary. This should not be too difficult, since most members of the graduate faculty are also members of the arts college faculty.

Mr. McGrath asks several pertinent questions, which are justified in view of "the present patternless mosaic in the— liberal arts college." For emphasis each of these questions is listed separately below.

"Can a set of generally acceptable objectives for liberal education be rediscovered?"

"Are there, in fact, any principles on the basis of which unity can be restored to liberal education?"

"Can the public generally assume that the graduates of liberal arts colleges possess certain knowledge, intellectual abilities and traits of character which may be considered the attributes of a cultivated mind and a cultured life?"[4]

Perhaps an attempt to answer these questions briefly would serve as the best means of summarizing the essential ideas in this and other chapters.

The answer to the first question is relatively easy. Mr.

[3] Earl J. McGrath, *The Graduate School and the Decline of Liberal Education*, Bureau of Publications, Teachers College, Columbia University, p. 13.
[4] *Ibid.*, p. 13.

McGrath has himself produced an excellent statement of the broad purposes of liberal education:

(1) to provide that comprehensive body of knowledge in the major branches of learning—the physical sciences, the social sciences, and the humanities, including the fine arts—without which the individual may be victimized by his own ignorance or by those who seek to bend his actions to their own purposes, (2) to cultivate the skill of reasoning and communication required to attack a new problem effectively, to order the relevant data, and to express by voice and by hand the results of these intellectual activities, and (3) to nurture the traits of mind and spirit characteristic of those who have achieved a consistent view of themselves and the complex physical and social world in which they live.

Few would find such objectives unacceptable, but to achieve them through the curriculum and methods of instruction is the difficult task. A curriculum built around ideas and their background rather than facts, and around ideals or motivations rather than events, has a chance to achieve the broad purposes of liberal education outlined by Mr. McGrath. Likewise, instructional methods that involve not only facts but the meaning of facts, not only knowledge but understanding, not only analysis but synthesis, are designed "to cultivate the skills of reasoning and communication required to attack a new problem effectively" and "to nurture the traits of mind and spirit characteristic of those who have achieved a consistent view of themselves and the complex physical and social world in which they live." This is the type of curriculum and of instruction contemplated in the graduate and undergraduate program focused on the significant ideals, concepts, and motivations that are the foundations of our way of life as set forth in this and the two preceding chapters.

The second question raised by Mr. McGrath is whether there are "any principles on the basis of which unity can be restored to liberal education." Again, the program just referred to would provide these principles. In such a program *meaning* of facts rather than facts becomes the primary goal; *understanding* rather than mere knowledge, the governing purpose; and *synthesis*, as well as analysis, as a requirement of the learner.

The third question is whether the public can assume that

the graduates of liberal arts colleges are in fact liberally educated. Under the present system no common body of knowledge nor a common approach to learning is to be found among college graduates. It is possible for two college graduates who have been awarded the B.A. degree in the same institution to have had no courses in common, save perhaps freshman English. The vast increase in knowledge, specialized and fragmented, has resulted in proliferation of college courses because there are no criteria for the selection of subject matter. In any case, acquiring knowledge of events is less important than understanding the motivation of those events.

The proposed program should insure that all college graduates have a common background of knowledge and understanding, and a common attitude toward learning. This is one of the major goals of the program as suggested earlier, because the body of significant ideals and concepts is more limited than the body of knowledge, the approach of this program should aid in reducing the number of undergraduate courses and in avoiding trivial subject matter. Again, in the study of fundamental ideas and ideals in the humanities and social sciences and of the significant developments in the natural sciences, the sense of values of the learner should be strengthened. Thus, in a variety of ways the new program assists in the solution of the problems of liberal education.

CHAPTER 8

The Ph.D. and
Preparation for Teaching

The Doctor of Philosophy degree in the United States has a unique status. For the profession of college teaching it is the union card. With rare exceptions a teacher cannot rise to the top without it. But government, business, and industry also hold it in high esteem and employ almost one half of those produced by the universities each year. They could use many more if they were available; indeed, much of the research they require is done by professors in the universities. If the number of doctorates who do not enter college and university teaching were added to those on campuses engaged in governmental, business, and industrial research and consultation, the remainder who devote their energies exclusively to teaching and to non-sponsored research would probably constitute a minority of the group.

The reasons for the strong and growing demand for Ph.D. graduates are many; they are different in the different agencies that seek them. Some analysis of these reasons will throw light on why the degree has such high prestige.

Educational institutions seeking recognition by the accrediting agencies must have a reasonable proportion of their staffs with maximum training. Hence, colleges on the way up have no alternative: they must seek Ph.D. graduates to man their classrooms and laboratories. Otherwise they will not be recognized. This is an arbitrary standard which harks back to the early history of accrediting associations, when some measure of the quality of the teaching staff had to be found. It is as arbitrary in insuring quality of teaching as high school units and college credits are in determining quality of education in schools and colleges—and it is as fixed. In such cases the Ph.D. is chiefly a symbol.

Whether or not the education pursued in acquiring the degree fitted the holder for instruction in a liberal arts college seems to carry little weight. The title is the important consideration. In 1895 and in the early nineteen-hundreds, when the accrediting associations were formed, there were no Ph.D.'s in agriculture, engineering, business administration, home economics, or music. Ph.D.'s were almost, if not quite exclusively, confined to the basic subjects, such as history, English, Latin, Greek, philosophy, or mathematics. Even though the majority of Ph.D.'s in many universities are awarded in other than the basic subjects, the tradition still prevails that the Ph.D. is evidence of good quality of instruction in a college faculty.

In the stronger colleges, which might insist that members of their teaching staffs acquire their Ph.D.'s in some liberal arts subject, little or no question is raised as to whether the kind of research pursued constitutes good or bad training for teaching the fundamentals in an arts college. Although everyone recognizes that the specialized research frequently required for the highest degree may contribute little or nothing to one's future effectiveness as a teacher, yet the Ph.D. is still essential in institutions large and small. The tradition is entrenched in spite of frequent complaints against specialization in preparation for college teaching.

In the strong universities the research required of the Ph.D. candidate is specific training for the work he will be expected to perform as an instructor and professor in that university or in some other. Hence, all universities, as a matter of course, require the kind of research and graduate work that they expect the neophyte to perpetuate.

A different set of reasons motivates government, business, and industry to seek men and women with the maximum training.

The scientific and technological research that produced anti-biotics, that made radar so important a factor in modern life, that gave us radio and television, and that startled the world by the production of the atomic bomb, were conducted, for the most part, by Ph.D.'s. The non-educational agencies saw that the key to progress was through research, and that the Doctor of Philosophy degree indicated training in that activity. In short, they are seeking those trained in research because they believe that it holds the key to their future progress.

The meaning of the degree becomes more and more confused as the number awarded increases in response to expanding demands. In 1900 there were 382 doctorates awarded; in 1940, a total of 3,290; and eighteen years later, in 1958, 8,942.[1] At the beginning of the century the number of subject fields in which this degree was awarded was limited; in 1958 the number had risen to sixty, besides a number of unnamed miscellaneous fields.

Among the new subjects that have been added to the original group of basic ones are agriculture, commerce and business administration, engineering, music, home economics, physical education, library, and social work. The degree has become the symbol of at least three years of advanced work beyond the bachelor's degree. There is no semblance of unity in the subject matter covered in the course work, in the kind of research pursued, in the objective of the training, or in the quality of the work. Departments in the same institution vary widely in their goals and in their requirements. Indeed, in the same department individual professors differ in what they expect of the Ph.D. candidate. Not only chaos but "amiable anarchy," as Barzun describes it, is characteristic of the Ph.D. program in American higher education. The degree actually has less meaning than the B.A.; that is to say, there is more variation in content, in standards, and in quality of work. This is not true of the well-established graduate school, though the situation even there leaves something to be desired.

[1] *American Universities and Colleges* (8th ed.; American Council on Education, 1960).

Though the Ph.D. is still the prestige degree in American universities, its currency has suffered from the lack of uniformity in quality, from the lag permitted between the B.A. and the Ph.D., and from the triviality of topics sometimes used for the dissertation. It can suffer the fate of the B.A. and the M.A., which have undoubtedly been seriously devalued in the past few decades.

The Ph.D. fetish is an American phenomenon. It is not encountered elsewhere in the university world in the form it has taken here. As already suggested, it derived originally from the unique American method of accrediting colleges and has persisted, despite its obvious weakness, probably because accrediting must continue as long as new institutions are being established. The method of insuring quality of work in the Commonwealth (English-speaking) countries is through affiliation of the new institutions with established universities, as university colleges, until such time as the new institution appears to the affiliating university to be qualified to operate independently. The matter of advanced degrees is not emphasized. First-class honors in the B.A. carries more weight than an M.A. or in some instances, a Ph.D. As a result, the shortage of college teachers is not so acute, especially in the humanities and the social sciences.

It is possible to provide college teaching personnel in the United Kingdom and in other Commonwealth areas from the ranks of those who have taken an honors degree (first class), because the nature and quality of the work required for the first-class honors degree are so well established. The lack of such fixed standards for the B.A. in American institutions results in advanced degrees being considered an essential requirement.

Since all would agree that college and university teachers should have the highest academic training if higher education is to fulfill its mission, no one is disposed to settle for less than the Ph.D. as standard preparation for teaching at the highest levels. Indeed, all suggestions for a new kind of doctor's degree—such as Doctor of Humanities, Doctor of Social Sciences, or Doctor of Science—have been generally rejected, since these would likely be second-class doctorates. Though the Doctor of Education is well established and awarded by many excellent institutions, it is not generally considered on a par with the Ph.D. Americans will not be willing to approve any second-class doctorate as standard preparation for membership in college faculties. This is true despite the fact that in many quarters there is deep dissatisfaction with the Ph.D. as well as with the master's and bachelor's degrees, which are the foundation upon which the Ph.D. structure rests.

The basic discontent arises from the lack of unity in each of the three degree programs. In the preceding chapter the absence of a common curriculum content for the B.A. degree was pointed out. Similarly, the M.A. degree varies in content and purpose, as already described.

Obviously, there must be great variety in the researches pursued by graduate students, for specialized training in many fields is required by American society, but in the preparation for college teaching surely there should be some common core of subject matter and some common purposes in instruction. How can this be achieved? is the basic question. Since knowledge is so vast in all fields, on what principle can subject matter be selected for the arts college curriculum and, therefore, for the research and study of those who are preparing to man the college classrooms and laboratories?

The answer to that question is inherent in the plans outlined in chapters V, VI, and VII, as they relate to the humanities, the social sciences, and the natural sciences. If, in the humanities and the social sciences, attention were focused on the significant ideas and goals that have evolved in the history of Western civilization, and on the ways in which these have influenced the quality and stability of our society, it should be possible to develop a core curriculum in the college that would serve admirably the ends of liberal education. This would give a unity to the B.A. curriculum that is now lacking. If the research of the Ph.D. candidate were directed toward discovering and formulating, one by one, the basic concepts that underlie our culture, it would be not only inherently worth while but specific preparation for teaching in a college of liberal arts.

In the natural sciences the same principle might be applied. In addition to the classroom and laboratory work required in a given science discipline, great emphasis would be placed upon the significant discoveries in that discipline, how they were arrived at and what their influence had been on the development of that and other sciences. Such an approach should be able to stir the imagination of the student, give new vitality to the study of the subject and greater understanding of its importance. All this should improve the motivation of the non-science majors and, at the same time, give the science majors an invaluable background for their work. It would be the kind of preparation for teaching science in college that would contribute directly to the advancement of liberal education.

The B.A. graduate whose study as an undergraduate dealt with the fundamental concepts and ideals that find expression in our literature, history, economics, and political science would be well prepared to proceed to a scholarly master's degree and from there to the doctorate. The unifying principle of the entire program of higher education for the seven years from high school graduation to the Ph.D. for those who plan to teach in college, would be concern for understanding the basic ideals and concepts and their influence upon our culture, and the role of science, its significant developments, and the meaning of the scientific method.

Only the academically gifted students should be encouraged to plan on graduate work, but all college undergraduates could profit by this program, for it should not be beyond the reach of any student qualified to enter college. The approach in the study would be the same, for the content would largely be the same. This would give a unity to the arts college which it now lacks, and would provide the basic liberal education which has traditionally been the aim of the college.

Under this plan admission to the second degree should be more restricted than it is at present. Preparation for it should normally begin in the junior year. The thesis for the master's degree might involve research on some one or more central concepts. If it be in history, the investigation might focus on the origin and development of the concept (or concepts), its influence on social progress, and its manifestation in our current outlook. If it be in literature, the research might involve studying the great literature of the past and present to find the extent to which the concept had affected the thinking of essayists, poets, and dramatists. If the degree be sought in a foreign language and literature, the process might be the same as for an English major, though presumably the literature would be studied in its own language.

In sociology, economics, and political science the emphasis might be upon the basic concepts and ideals that underlie social, economic, and political institutions and their influence on modern society. It is not enough to comprehend the complex maze of institutions that go to make up our society; it is more important to know the motivations that gave them birth and that have nurtured them through the years. What a wealth of material is at hand for master's theses and doctoral dissertations. One who had spent three years delving into the backgrounds of our culture, seeking to understand its motivations, would be more likely to have a zest for teaching fundamentals to youth in a college classroom than one whose research had involved detailed investigation in some highly specialized and restricted area largely unrelated to the life around him.

What distinction could be made between the doctor's degree based on this program of instruction and research and the one now given? The degree awarded might be the Doctor of Philosophy abbreviated as D.Phil. There is a precedent for it, at Oxford, the oldest of Anglo-Saxon universities, where it is the most advanced research degree given. If candidates for this degree were required to take the honors master's degree—which might be styled the M.Phil. to distinguish it from the ordinary M.A.— it would have prestige from the start; and with the high degree of selection for the M.Phil., which would be a necessary stepping-stone to the D.Phil., the standard could be kept high. Thus, training for teaching in colleges and universities could be made superior to that required for the ordinary Ph.D. This in itself would tend to attract the ablest students, who would be challenged by it. By the same token, the teaching profession could be exalted by making preparation for it the most advanced work offered by the university.

There would also be a symbolic significance to this change in the style of the degree. The Ph.D. represents the highest achievement under the system of education borrowed from the Germans. If the new program reverted to the English degree, it would suggest that the German philosophy of graduate education was being replaced or supplemented by the British which, after all, was originally based on the *studium generale* rather than on the technical, professional, and specialized type of education found in the German universities. In fact, the shift in the program involves just that kind of change. In the undergraduate and graduate work in the basic fields, the broad philosophical approach is proposed. It would involve a complete integration of the university program of instruction and research in the three broad divisions of knowledge—the humanities, the social sciences, and the natural sciences—and would effect a natural articulation between the undergraduate and the graduate years in the basic fields.

The doctor's degree for the technical, technological, and professional fields could remain the Ph.D. In this way a distinction could be made between graduate work in these fields and graduate work in the fundamental subjects. Such a distinction would assist in solving the problem of reconciling the program of science and technology with the university tradition, which is discussed at some length in Chapter IV.

The great dialectical tradition of university education is concerned with fundamental issues. It is in the context of that tradition that the *pursuit of truth* was declared to be the primary goal of the university. Unless that tradition and ideal are preserved and nourished as chief objectives of the modern university, they can wither and die. It is of the utmost importance that they survive and prosper, for without them universities become little more than scientific, technological, or professional institutes.

This involves in the humanistic-social studies field basic research of a type different from that in the natural sciences. It would be concerned with values, with the fundamental ideals and motivations of our society.

In such a search for understanding the entire range of basic subjects would be covered—history and literature, domestic and foreign, ancient and modern; philosophy, psychology, economics, political science, and the natural sciences. This search would also lead to a consideration of the basic problems and issues of our time. A criticism of the modern university education is that it no longer asks the important questions or deals with fundamental issues. The approach here proposed would meet that criticism.

The changes in the methods of research and instruction suggested would have to be initiated by the graduate school, though the development of the program would require the collaboration of the college faculty. The process of modifying present procedures in both the undergraduate and the graduate divisions would require time. It could be effected only through prolonged and painstaking effort with the fullest cooperation of the central administration and all the faculties involved in instruction and research in the basic arts and science subjects. Much experimentation, checking results, and investigation will be required before such a change in program, but it should be possible to accomplish it gradually without disrupting the ongoing program of a university.

In view of the fundamental changes suggested both in curriculum and in method, the program should be tested out in a small group of universities which have an interest in it and which would be willing to conduct a serious five-year experiment in an effort to appraise its merits. Each participating institution should be working on criteria for the selection of significant ideas and concepts, acceptable topics for theses and dissertations, areas of investigation, seminar topics, graduate course requirements, the type of independent work that might be required in lieu of course work, etc.

Other matters requiring consideration of the graduate faculties might be the nature and scope of the comprehensive examination for admission to study for the doctor's degree, reading lists to be covered by those preparing for the qualifying examinations, the length of the dissertation and the examination on it. These and many other issues in graduate education should be reviewed by the institutions in the course of the experiment. A new pattern for independent work might emerge as these questions are reviewed and answered. Many believe that the amount of prescribed course work for the doctor's candidate is excessive because it tends to hamper the development of independent scholarly habits.

The students involved in the experimental program should be planning to proceed without delay to the Ph.D. They should be selected for the program not later than the junior year of college, be writing papers based on investigation as early as the first semester of the junior year, be required to pass the foreign language requirement for the Ph.D. by the end of the senior college year, and be prepared for the qualifying examination before the end of the first semester of the second year of graduate work.

Let us turn now to the matter of the Ph.D. program as preparation for teaching in a liberal arts college. Since the degree is awarded in more than sixty subject fields, it is obvious that all Ph.D. holders are not prepared for college teaching. Those who have acquired the degree in agriculture, engineering, pharmacy, medical sciences, and other professional fields would have no interest in or qualification for college teaching. Only those who have majored in some one of the basic subject fields should be considered for teaching posts in colleges.

In a recent volume of *Dissertation Abstracts* there is a listing of only nine topics in the entire field of history. There is no listing for English, but under "Language and Literature" there are six dissertations in English literature and, except under linguistics, none in American literature. Under the "Linguistics" section there are twelve subjects listed. On the other hand, a total of fourteen abstracts are recorded in the section entitled "Speech-Theater." Under "Philosophy" there are five.

In "Economics" the statistics are more encouraging. A total of thirty-three titles are listed, but the nature of the topics is discouraging. A few examples will illustrate: "The Economics of Price Discrimination," "The Concept of Disclosure on Financial Statements," "The Domestic Consumption of Rice in the United States," and finally "The Distribution of Gains from Advancing Productivity in some Concentrated and Non-Concentrated Industries."[2] The question here is not whether the topics are worthy of research for the Ph.D. or whether the dissertation is of high quality. Both the topics and the investigation carried out are doubtless thoroughly in keeping with university traditions. The question is rather whether the type of research required is satisfactory preparation for one who is planning to teach economics in a liberal arts college. In the main the investigations carried out on these topics concerned practical problems in the American economy valuable to business executives, but hardly relevant to the task of teaching economics as a liberal arts subject.

In contrast with the nine history, six English literature, and five philosophy topics, sixty-three topics were listed under "Education," forty-eight under "Engineering," and forty in "Agriculture." There is no reason to suppose that the July 1960 volume of *Dissertation Abstracts* is not typical.

The advanced training now given in professional fields is encouraging, but a comparison of it with the training in the humanistic-social studies fields is a matter for sober reflection. In graduate school circles the suggestion that the Ph.D. is a professional degree is anathema, heretical—and yet, in the light

[2] *Dissertation Abstracts* (Ann Arbor, Mich.: University Microfilms, Inc., 1960), XXI, No. 1.

of these facts, what can be said for the Ph.D. being free from professional bias? The leaders in graduate education appear to be unaware of the trends of recent decades, and of the extent to which the Ph.D. is now granted for work in professional schools; otherwise, they would be more willing to consider seriously the need for basic reforms. Surely recent trends in subject-matter fields and in thesis and dissertation topics and the general tone and quality of graduate education are to be viewed with apprehension.

This much is certain: the Ph.D. degree is no guarantee that its holder is qualified to give instruction in the liberal arts college. The nature of research performed even in the basic subjects is often unrelated to liberal education and, as such, is not satisfactory preparation for college teaching. Despite the fact that this is generally recognized as true, the Ph.D. is still sought after since there is no other program designed to fill the needs of the prospective teacher.

The D.Phil. degree is possibly the answer to the problem. It involves identifying the gifted student early, not later than the junior year in college; it requires a more rigorous program in the upper two years of college and the first year of graduate work; the type of research, which deals with significant ideas and concepts, is better suited as preparation for college teaching; and in the final two years the rigor of the requirements for the doctorate will insure better research and instruction than that in the Ph.D. program. This means that the D.Phil. should be superior to the usual Ph.D. in every respect and particularly as preparation for college teaching.

This is as it should be, for college and university teaching must be able to command the best minds and the best training that society can provide if higher education is to fulfill its mission and if the agencies that must rely upon its services are to prosper. Nothing is more vital to American stability and progress than the quality, preparation, and dedication of its college and university teaching and research personnel. This means that the graduate schools, which must recruit, educate and inspire this vast army, have the major responsibility for meeting this challenge. I am convinced that neither the graduate schools, nor the government, nor business and industry, nor educational leaders, nor the general public have realized fully how strategic a role the graduate schools must play in the educational crisis that faces us, if we are to rise to the challenge of the next two or three decades.

The most far-reaching and wisest reforms within graduate education itself are essential, but these alone will not suffice. Financial support for these agencies of society, in far larger amounts than have been dreamed of hitherto, will be required. As a matter of national health, welfare, safety, and progress, no superior mind should be allowed to remain undeveloped for lack of a chance to secure maximum training; yet a large proportion of the most gifted are lost to further training in high schools and colleges. The climate of opinion in the American community should not allow this to take place. If the reason is lack of motivation on the part of the individual, that may be the fault of the public attitude. If lack of funds to attend college keeps out many able students, this ought to be remedied by a combination of local, state, and national efforts. If the sense of values in the home or in the community, or in both, are responsible for drop-outs at the secondary school and college levels, the schools and community leaders should take steps to remedy the situation.

It is in this perspective that we must view the importance of recruiting and training our most gifted, as well as our least gifted and average, young people. The high school and the college teacher and, above all, the university teacher have a primary responsibility for recruiting and challenging the able students. In view of the critical times in which we live and the struggle for intellectual superiority which is occurring in the international sphere, the accent must be on the gifted and on search for talent if we hope to prevail.

CHAPTER 9

The Growing Deficit in Ph.D's.—
Its Causes and Its Remedy

The growth of the college population in the United States is the marvel of this century: from 238,000 in round figures, in 1900, to 2,300,000 in 1950, to 3,600,000 in 1960. While the census figures indicate a population increase from 75,000,000 to 150,000,000, college and university enrollments increased tenfold. Though this expansion has no counterpart elsewhere, it appears to be largely responsible for the vast growth of interest in higher education in other parts of the world since 1950 —as evidenced by the 50,000 foreign students now in American colleges and universities.

But the expansion of undergraduate enrollments during the first half of this century is small compared with that of graduate enrollments in the same period. While the colleges and university populations increased twentyfold, the graduate school expansion was fortyfold—from 5,800 in 1900 to 237,000 in 1950. Despite this increase, graduate education has by no means kept up with the needs. The shortage of trained personnel has been more keenly felt during the past decade than during any period in American history. The needs of colleges and universities for men and women to man classrooms and laboratories have been so great as to constitute a serious crisis.

In 1957 the President's Committee on Education Beyond the High School reported that estimates indicated the need for 15,000 to 25,000 Ph.D.'s each year for ten years; in the same year the universities were producing fewer than 9,000 Ph.D.'s, of whom only 5,000 were entering the teaching profession. Every year of the decade the decline in the proportion of Ph.D.'s available for filling college and university positions has accelerated. For example, from 1953 to 1958 the percentage of such Ph.D.'s dropped from 40 to 23 per cent. Since 1957 there has been a slight increase in the number of Ph.D.'s produced each year, but as this has been far from adequate to meet the growing demand, the percentage of those available with top training continues to drop steadily. Unless heroic efforts are made to check this cumulative deficit, it could prove disastrous. But shortage of teaching personnel is only one facet of the problem.

Government, business, and industry are clamoring for men and women with maximum training. Since World War II research has become a big business. The expeditures for research amounted in 1959 to twelve billion dollars, and in 1961 to sixteen billion.[1] Of these amounts the universities account for less than 4 per cent; the great bulk was spent by government and industry. A bulletin of the National Research Council issued in 1956 contained information on 4,834 industrial laboratories listed under 4,060 organizations. These laboratories are concerned with the advancement of knowledge, usually in specialized fields, but do not normally engage in instruction. They depend largely upon the universities for training their key personnel.

Thus, the demand for trained men and women required by government and industry is even greater than that of the universities for teaching staff. The crisis in graduate education, therefore, stems from the needs of both university and non-university agencies. The rapid increase in the number of college students since the war and the concurrent expansion of interest in research on the part of government and industry have combined to produce the most critical situation in higher education that has been experienced in this country.

A variety of efforts have been made to meet the demands. The Woodrow Wilson Fund of some twenty-five million dollars

[1] Government statistics.

was set up to assist in attracting able young men and women to graduate study, with particular reference to the need for college teachers. The National Defense Education Act of 1958 had much the same purpose in mind. Financial assistance for graduate work has been furnished by universities, foundations, institutes, councils, and scholarly and professional societies as well as by state and Federal governments, industrial and commercial organizations, individual donors, and other agencies.

A comparatively recent development is the establishment of research institutes within universities, usually for the purpose of promoting specific types of investigation. For example, the Ohio State University Research Foundation and the Purdue Research Foundation were established in order to advance industrial research. The Wisconsin Alumni Research Foundation, established to encourage scientific investigation, awards fellowships to students in the natural sciences and grants-in-aid to faculty members. The Institute of Research in the Social Sciences at the University of North Carolina is designed to advance research, to train personnel in social science investigation, and to coordinate regional activities in the social sciences. Among the Federal agencies that award fellowships for graduate study are the United States Public Health Service, the Office of Vocational Rehabilitation, and the National Science Foundation.

Even with these widespread efforts to induce gifted individuals to enter upon graduate work, the deficit in the production of Ph.D.'s and other qualified postgraduates, as compared with the need, seems to be growing. This situation raises the question as to why the higher education system should be failing to meet the demand. Perhaps it is due in part to the explosion of interest in research on the part of government, business, and industry and the concurrent expansion of college enrollments, which requires more teachers, but this answer provides little comfort when little or no perceptible progress is being made toward solving the problem. It suggests that reforms may be needed in our university methods and procedures.

Concern for the future is enhanced by the fact that new discoveries and new knowledge continue to open up new vistas of need and of opportunity which will increase the demand for advanced studies and research. If one examines the situation closely, it would appear that graduate education and research may still be in their infancy, that their great expansion is yet to come. Research in the fields of nuclear physics, outer space, radar, radio astronomy, human genetics, and molecular biology seems to be in a relatively early stage of development.

Another fact worthy of consideration in this connection is that while progress in the biological and physical sciences is constantly opening up new areas of investigation, little basic work is as yet being done in the social sciences and the humanities. Though the current emphasis is upon the natural sciences and technology, there is a growing realization of the need for basic investigation in the humanistic-social studies areas.

The increasing complexity of modern society, the growing individual and collective tensions resulting, in part at least, from the changes imposed by an advancing science and technology, and the conflicts in human relations which charaterize our age, all point to the imperative need for basic study and research in these fields. Ours is not only a scientific and technological but an ideological age as well. It may well be that in the long run the discovery of new knowledge about human motivation, aspiration, and organization will be more important in achieving international leadership than superiority in the natural sciences and technology.

In view of the manifest need for greater emphasis on the science of human relations, and the emerging recognition of this need, it is possible that within the next twenty-five years the demand for advanced work, including research, in this area may eclipse that of science and technology which now claims the lion's share of the budget and the interest of the most gifted youth. Just as medicine, which for many years attracted the ablest young people of this country, has now yielded first place to science and technology, so in time it is not inconceivable that humanistic-social studies will supplant the physical and biological sciences in attracting talented youth.

After all, the humanities constituted the central core of university education for many centuries before the advent of scientific and technological studies. Because they are concerned with the fundamental problems of man and his society, they cannot continue to be neglected. Their rebirth will not take place, however, simply by a reshuffling of traditional subject matters or even by strengthening the current curriculums in anthropology, sociology, economics, political science, and philosophy. It will require pioneering research, designed to effect a breakthrough that will remove the shackles of the outmoded traditionalism and the pseudo-scientific approach which have been largely responsible for the present unhappy plight of the humanities and the social sciences. As this problem was dealt with in some detail in earlier chapters, it will suffice here to call attention to it as an element in the graduate study demands of the future.

In the light of these facts, what are the prospects for graduate study in the next twenty-five years? The Heald Committee's report, on the needs of higher education in the State of New York by 1985, predicted more than a threefold increase in enrollments over the 1960 figure—from 425,000 to 1,270,000.[2] Assuming a similar expansion in the country as a whole in that period, the college and university populations would be in excess of 10,000,000 by 1985. Of that number how many would be graduate students? As a basis for an estimate, a comparison of undergraduate and graduate enrollments for the first half of the century might be useful.

A glance at this table reveals that expansion of graduate students was five times greater than that of the over-all enrollment of higher education in the first half of the century. A projection of those figures, which tripled the college and university population, would produce for 1985 a figure for graduate students of more than 4,000,000. If the percentage of graduate students

[2] Report to Governor Rockefeller on Higher Education, November 1960.

TABLE 4[3]

College & University Enrollments		Graduate School Enrollments
1900	237,592	5,831
1910	355,000	9,370
1920	597,000	15,612
1930	1,100,000	47,255
1940	1,494,000	106,119
1950	2,296,592	237,600
1960	3,600,000 (Est.)	305,000

[3] *American Universities and Colleges* (8th ed.; American Council on Education, 1960).

should remain the same as in 1960, the graduate population would be approximately 1,000,000. Based on these and other facts, a conservative estimate of graduate student enrollment by 1985 would be about 2,000,000. This means that the proportion of graduate students to undergraduates would have doubled in the twenty-five years since 1960, which is not an unwarranted assumption.

Berelson's study shows that the number of Ph.D.'s grew from 394 in 1908 to 8,942 in 1958. In the past thirty years there has been a sixfold increase—47,255 to 305,000—in the number of graduate students. If the same rate of growth should continue, by 1988 the number of Ph.D.'s awarded annually would be 53,657. But during the period from 1928 to 1958 the population in the United States more than doubled, while the increase from 1898 to 1928 was scarcely 60 per cent. This means that the number of Ph.D.'s should grow faster from 1958 to 1988 than in the previous thirty-year period. On that basis 53,657 is likely to be on the low side.

The large increase since 1928 in the number of Ph.D.'s needed by government, business, and industry also suggests that the figure is conservative. The fact that there is a great deficit in Ph.D.'s is still further reason for considering 53,657 a low figure even for 1985.

Is this a realistic figure in the light of the need for advanced degrees? If 300,000 students enrolled in advanced studies produces 10,000 Ph.D.'s per year, 2,000,000 on the same basis should produce, in round figures, 65,000. The question that immediately arises is whether such numbers would be required.

The President's Committee on Education Beyond the High School reported the need for 15,000 to 25,000 a year over a ten-year period, at least, for college and university teachers, whereas only 5,000 were going into teaching each year, about half the number graduating. In order to provide 25,000 teachers a year the graduate schools should produce 50,000 Ph.D.'s annually. Since this number (25,000) was suggested by the President's Committee as possibly needed every year until 1970, beginning in 1957, and because the deficit has continued to increase since that time, an annual production of 65,000 Ph.D.'s by 1985 would probably not fill the needs that can now be envisioned. The rapidly growing requirements of government, business, and industry since 1950 for people with maximum training suggest that any forecast of what this demand will be in another twenty-five years is likely to be highly conservative.

The conclusion is convincing that, from the standpoint of need, 2,000,000 graduate students in the universities of the country by 1985 cannot be considered unrealistic. It is likely that such a number will be insufficient to meet the needs rather than that it will produce a surplus. An almost unlimited demand exists for graduate students prepared to man the laboratories of government and industry and to fill teaching posts in the universities. The fact is that industry is having to train on the job a large proportion of its scientists and technologists. If the universities continue to fail to supply the need, they may find that business, industry, and government will set up independent training programs—as, indeed, they have already begun to do in some instances.

I am not unaware of the reasoned conclusion in Berelson's recent study that there is no unusual need for doctorates. As pointed out earlier, this conclusion is based upon a series of false premises:

1. That all Ph.D.'s that enter educational instutions are going into teaching: whereas many go to agricultural experiment sta-

tions, medical schools, and engineering.

2. That 14 to 1 is the lowest pupil-teacher ratio to be expected: whereas 10 to 1 is more realistic.

3. That 10 per cent of the junior college teaching staff are Ph.D.'s is ample and all that will be required.

4. That no Ph.D.'s will be employed by secondary schools: whereas some physicists are saying that for proper instruction in secondary schools a Ph.D. is required.

5. That no significant number of doctorates go into public school administration.

6. That the present 40 per cent of four-year college teaching staffs are Ph.D.'s is adequate.

7. That the decline in the number of Ph.D.'s available to fill college vacancies is insignificant: whereas between 1953 and 1958 it went from nearly 40 to 23 per cent.

8. That there is no need to be concerned about upgrading the quality of instruction in our universities.

Perhaps the most serious assumption of all in the Berelson study is that the quality of Ph.D. work is satisfactory because a majority of the faculty and a still larger percentage of recent graduates, college presidents, and business representatives are satisfied with it. It is natural that those who are closely connected with an enterprise should be reasonably satisfied with it.

The late Abraham Flexner found the same situation in the medical schools of the country when he made his famous study early in the second decade of this century. He was fond of relating his experience with one university president who was so satisfied with his medical school program that he felt no need for the substantial help that Mr. Flexner was prepared to recommend for his institution. (He never made the recommendation.) If a poll of faculty members, presidents, and recent graduates of medical schools in 1912 had been taken, it would doubtless have revealed reasonable satisfaction with the status quo—on the part of all these groups. Yet when the public became aware of the real situation through the study, great dissatisfaction prevailed.

There is already public concern about the effectiveness of graduate education. This has been true for twenty years but has been much more acute during the last five to ten years than at any other period. Educational leaders not now involved in graduate education, and many who are, have expressed great dissatisfaction with the inefficiency of the current program.

The complacency expressed in some quarters about the present status of graduate education in the United States is difficult to justify in the light of the facts. In some respects the situation that now exists is comparable to that of medical education in 1912, when the Flexner report appeared. At that time the medical schools of the country were largely proprietary institutions with part-time professors. They had sprung up in response to community needs for doctors. They had no budgets. The professors, who lectured between operations or between home and hospital calls, agreed on some basis for splitting the tuition fees of their students. A secretary-treasurer was employed to collect fees and to distribute them. Admission standards were lax, and rigorous training was rare. Bright students often took the state board examinations before completing the course, passed them, and practiced a year or two before returning for the M.D. degree. Others worked part-time while attending medical school. The capable ones were often able, on this part-time arrangement, to complete the course in the prescribed time. Others spread their training over several years. In those days the study of medicine was often a casual matter. After the training, or even before it was completed, one might take the state board examination and, if successful, enter practice immediately. If he failed, he might repeat the examination as many times as he wished. Some were lost to the profession for lack of ability to outguess the examiners after repeated attempts. When one recalls the present rigorous standards of medical education, it is difficult to conceive how different the situation was only a few decades ago.

With these facts in mind, let us take a look at graduate education in 1961. Proprietary institutions still exist that offer the Ph.D. degree. Recently in India someone questioned the author about these institutions, one of which had victimized a friend of his. Within the past few years these bogus degree mills have been so active as to arouse the ire and the action of the American Council on Education. It has sent out a "Suggested State Legislation Program for 1961" urging states to outlaw them.

The reader may feel that reference to degree mills has no place in a discussion of graduate education, because they are not a part of it but are a monstrous hoax deplored by all. The reason for mentioning them is that such a situation exists only because leaders in higher education have not aroused public opinion and brought pressure on states to forbid such practices. It is hoped that the current efforts of the Council will be successful.

One of the chief recommendations of the 1912 medical study was that medical faculty members should have full-time status, and this has been the case for thirty years. While some remunerative practice is allowed, this is considered useful for keeping *au courant* with the profession. In the graduate schools part-time faculty is the pattern. As a matter of fact, these divisions of universities began as temporary arrangements for students who wanted to do advanced work. Departments of graduate education developed into schools which, like the early medical schools, still have no budgets, the faculty being paid through the departments of the college and the professional schools. Under the present organization in most universities, the graduate dean's recommendations and those of his council can be ignored by departments with impunity. The dean's status reminds one of the secretary-treasurer of the proprietary medical schools of 1912, so far as his administrative authority is concerned.

The medical student who spread his study for the M.D. degree over several years, working part-time to make expenses or dropping out to practice a year or so, has many counterparts in the graduate schools of today. It has been argued that it is good for the graduate student to teach awhile before going on to the Ph.D. That same argument was used by medical students fifty years ago. To practice medicine for a year or more before taking the M.D. degree enabled the student to appreciate more fully the advanced courses. But you never hear such a suggestion any more. Neither the state laws nor the medical schools will permit it.

In many respects the same casual attitude that prevailed toward the study of medicine in the early part of this century, still prevails with respect to graduate studies. The result is an inexcusable lag between the B.A. and the Ph.D. Yet there are those who regard the situation as reasonably satisfactory.

To meet the future demands for graduate education, the present university organization is inadequate. In the preceding chapters the basis of this statement has been analyzed in some detail. In addition, the solution of some of the problems has been suggested, and a program outlined for strengthening graduate education in the United States. The inertia of tradition and long-established custom, backed by the vested interests of departmental autonomy, will be natural barriers to change, but they will not permanently block needed reforms, provided the situation is clearly understood and the alternatives are well conceived and planned.

The faculties of universities have demonstrated on many occasions their ability to adapt procedures to meet new demands, as reforms in medical, legal, theological, engineering, and nursing education so amply illustrate. Perhaps the most radical departure from tradition was effected when graduate and research work became central to the university purpose, a movement that began with the founding of Johns Hopkins. The incorporation of the land-grant college program in American higher education is another example of change to which the faculties became adjusted, though not without a long and difficult struggle. If one recalls the series of departures from tradition which has characterized the evolution of American higher education, he is not likely to insist that basic reforms in the graduate school organization and procedure are impossible. If graduate schools are given the responsibility, opportunity, and authority for effecting the basic changes needed, I have no doubt about the results.

CHAPTER 10

Summary Appraisal
of the Graduate Program

As a backdrop for the critical appraisal of the present graduate program, let us review briefly its merits, the significance of its present and future role, and the debt we owe to research and graduate work developed in the universities and directed by the graduate schools.

The prestige of the Ph.D. is a tribute to the standards maintained by graduate schools. The growing demand for men and women who have achieved this degree is still further evidence of the high quality of the advanced work sponsored by graduate schools. The fact, however, that the demand far outruns the supply is a matter of concern.

The indications are that graduate education is on the eve of its greatest expansion. The number of divisions of the university requiring maximum training of their teachers has increased markedly in the past decade, and they are providing candidates for the doctorate in far greater numbers. At the same time the relative number of Ph.D. holders available as instructors in the various arts college subjects is declining alarmingly. This means that the demands of the colleges and universities are far from being met. Concurrently the clamor for Ph.D.'s on the part of government, business, and industry is equally great. To fill the already acute need will become more difficult as higher education enrollments and the demands of other agencies increase. Unless the graduate schools are to fail utterly to meet the rising tide of expectation and need, they must gird themselves for a new and far more strategic role than they have played to date. This seems an inevitable conclusion, if one takes careful inventory of the variety of factors and pressures that are involved.

This is not to disparage past contributions of graduate education. The universities, through their programs of advanced study and research, have contributed incomparably to the social, economic, and industrial progress of the nation. By pointing the way to progress through research they have provided a new outlook to the professions, to government, to business and industry, and to the man in the street who has a new confidence in education as a result of the miracles performed by science and technology. In short, the universities have made Americans, at all levels and in all walks of life, *research-conscious*. The effect of this on American progress is incalculable.

It is with these facts in mind that I would like to examine the shortcomings, the needs—the unfinished business still on the agenda of graduate education. With its merits, its achievements, and especially its future possibilities as a background, the needs for improvement may stand out all the more clearly.

One of the most glaring defects in graduate education is its weakness in recruitment of talent. Someone has said that the medical student decides on his profession by the time he finishes high school, that the prospective lawyer makes up his mind usually in his sophomore or junior year, but that the future college teacher will have completed undergraduate work and frequently his master's degree before deciding to go on to the Ph.D. This accounts, in part at least, for the high attrition rate in graduate schools and the distressing gap between the B.A. and the Ph.D. Several factors have a part to play in this delay, including the variation in the time that may be required for acquiring the degree; the indefiniteness of the program leading to it, and the indifference on the part of college faculty members toward suggesting that students might follow in their footsteps. But the lack of any systematic recruitment plan is perhaps the chief factor. Such a program should begin not later than the beginning of the junior year and would be still more effective if it began in the first college year.

The Woodrow Wilson Fund and the National Defense Education Act fellowships have been useful in attracting gifted students into the profession, but since they are not presented until toward the end of the senior year many are not psychologically conditioned to the idea of becoming a college professor. In any case, other choices are presented much earlier. Business administration and engineering, for example, have undergraduate programs and thus begin recruiting among high school seniors and continue through the freshman and sophomore years. Premedical, prelegal, prenursing, and other preprofessional groups provide for recruitment using both faculty and students. No such organization interested in college teaching as a profession exists. Why shouldn't there be a *pregraduate* group of gifted students chosen by the faculty and pointed early toward graduate work. Such groups should make it far easier to identify promising prospective college teachers and prepare them early psychologically for the task.

The fact is that there is little or no articulation between college and graduate education. They are, as it were, in separate compartments. The one may qualify for admission to the other but rarely prepares for it. The university idea of scholarship is not presented systematically either before or after the award of the B.A.; and yet it could be introduced effectively as early as the junior year. There is actually no well-organized program of preparation for graduate work. In most institutions at least, if anything is done to help a student to get ready for graduate study, it is usually only a haphazard effort. This results in great loss of time on the part of students who enter graduate work, and, doubtless, in loss of talent, too, for if able students were identified early and encouraged to look forward to advanced work and to prepare for it, many who now drop out of the university on receiving the B.A. or go into other professions might be recruited for college teaching.

The college faculty should collaborate with the graduate school in identifying and challenging talented students. In some respects the greatest weakness in higher education is its failure to challenge the best efforts of the ablest students. The academically gifted are often the most neglected group on the campus. The weak student, in danger of failing, comes in for counsel; the average student, active in student life, has many contacts with deans of students and faculty advisers of student organizations, but the talented, scholarly student often has the least contact with the faculty in his undergraduate years, especially in institutions where there is a low premium on scholastic excellence.

The character of the master's degree in most universities is not such as to build respect for graduate work. As already pointed out, in some institutions the first graduate degree is essentially only a fifth year of undergraduate work; in others it is a consolation prize for those who have been unsuccessful in the Ph.D. qualifying examinations; and in still others it is a professional degree for those planning to teach in the public schools. Undergraduates are vaguely aware of these defects in the first graduate degree. The result is that the able student is not attracted to graduate study. There are some institutions that require two years of scholarly work for this degree, but since there are so few of these, they do not affect materially the picture sketched above.

Another factor that discourages the best students from considering graduate work is the great lag between the B.A. and the Ph.D. Most undergraduate students know people who have been struggling for the Ph.D. for years; many have teachers who have completed all requirements for the degree except the dissertation. The uncertainty about the degree is a real deterrent. Able students will respond to the challenge of rigorous requirements but not to uncertainty. It is a disturbing fact that the graduate school, which should attract the ablest students, has developed practices and procedures that tend to drive away the best-equipped and most capable students. How many applicants would there be for medical schools if the average length of time between the B.A. and the M.D. were seven to twelve years? The medical school admits only those students who plan on four consecutive years, and if one drops out for any reason except health, he is not likely to be readmitted. The result is that 85 to 90 per cent receive the M.D. within four years. Having been carefully selected, the medical student knows that if he does his part, he will reach his goal in the allotted time. The requirements are stiff, but the result is reasonably certain.

There is no doubt that the vagueness of requirements, the laissez-faire attitude of the graduate school, and the uncertainty of finally receiving the Ph.D. have been serious stumbling blocks to attracting really capable students to graduate study. Three major reasons are usually assigned for the long lapse of time between the B.A. and the Ph.D.: (1) students have to work to finance advanced study; (2) they need teaching experience before coming up for the Ph.D.; and (3) since special research ability is required for the advanced degree, it is impossible to say with certainty that even a carefully selected student has what it takes. Let us examine briefly each of these reasons.

Most graduate students do have difficulty financing graduate education; so do medical students. More fellowship funds are available for graduate than for medical students, the cost of the course per year is far less, and the number of years required is three instead of four. The argument that teaching for a while before coming up for the final degree is equally weak. Fifty years ago such an argument was used in medicine, and students sometimes took the state medical board examinations after three years and practiced awhile before taking the M.D. Finally, the suggestion is nonsense that the graduate student has to have some esoteric talent, not easily discoverable, which makes for uncertainty as to whether or when he can secure the Ph.D.

The real reasons for the situation in graduate education are: (1) that the goals and purposes of graduate study have not been clarified; (2) the steps by which the student may prepare himself for the foreign language and qualifying examinations have not been clearly stated; (3) the selection of the dissertation topic is often delayed; (4) individual faculty members may delay unduly the approval of the topic and the dissertation itself; and (5) there is a general laxness in pushing the candidate on to the completion of his work. The unnecessary delays and uncertainties connected with the Ph.D. program are serious obstacles to attracting able students and to the production of Ph.D. graduates.

A series of problems cluster around the dissertation. There is no consensus among graduate faculties as to its purpose, its optimum length, the amount of supervision its writer should have, or the nature of the topic that should be chosen. Is the purpose to make an original contribution to knowledge, or a report on research performed, or a demonstration of the student's ability to do research and report on it adequately? Or might it be a literary production (in the humanities) indicating genuine creative ability? What length should it be? Scientific and mathematical dissertations will be shorter than those in the humanistic-social science fields, but the range is fantastic. One dissertation in a land-grant university was twenty-six pages in length; another contained one thousand pages of typewritten material. Dean Elder of Harvard suggests that the experience of writing a dissertation prepares one for writing neither a book nor a good article. Confusion prevails over the extent to which the candidate should be supervised in his research and writing. Some professors leave the student alone unless he asks for help; others follow the work of a student so closely that his initiative is cramped. The individual professor often follows a method that suits his schedule and temperament, which may vary sharply from that of his colleague in the same department. One who may wish to present a piece of creative writing as a thesis is usually disappointed, though occasionally such a plan is approved. Lack of systematic planning, of approved criteria, of collective responsibility, and of common individual standards in faculty groups results in a feeling of insecurity on the part of both the faculty and the student, which seriously handicaps the progress of graduate education in American universities.

Related to this matter of criteria and standards is the problem of the lack of organized collective responsibility on the part of the graduate faculty. In all university divisions except the graduate school, the collective judgment of the faculty under whom one studies determines whether or not he passes and receives his degree, or fails. Insofar as one's course work is concerned in the graduate school, the same policy prevails. But in the research work in graduate education, the judgment of a single faculty member may often determine the fate of a student. This appears to influence considerably the attrition rate and is often responsible for the delay in achieving the degree. If it is proper that collective faculty judgment should determine whether one is awarded the B.A., the LL.B., or the M.D. degrees, why should the system be different for one seeking the Ph.D. degree? While admission to study for the doctorate is determined by a committee, the research topic, how and when it is selected, and the nature of the research performed are determined usually by a single faculty member. As already suggested, individual faculty members differ markedly in their judgments and in their requirements. This produces a variability in a given faculty that is difficult to justify.

If we look at the graduate education enterprise as a whole, with its three hundred thousand-odd students, it would appear to deserve better organization, a more effective system of appraising quality, and a more systematic method of operation. As we contemplate a doubling or a tripling of present numbers in the next fifteen to twenty years, it appears all the more imperative that the organization and method of operation of graduate schools should be tightened and girded for action as the most important single segment of America's system of higher education.

The qualifying examination and preparation for it are in a state of confusion. The graduate departments in many cases have never defined for themselves, much less for the students, what ground the examination should cover and how to go about preparing for it. In many institutions there is no syllabus or bibliography of reading for the students. Indeed, if they had the bibliography and did not know what the purpose or the scope of the examination would be, they would be little better off. Students have been known to flounder for two years or more in the attempt to get ready for these examinations, without knowing what they were preparing for. Surely the time has come when graduate faculty members should give serious thought to the qualifying examination and should clarify its nature and scope for themselves and for the students.

Such clarification would be no small task. It would be necessary to define the areas with which the student should be acquainted so far as his department is concerned; more than that, there are general areas of which each student should have some knowledge and for which he could prepare. The object of the examination is, of course, to determine how broad a background the student has, how fully he has grasped the important ideas, and how clearly he can think about them. In a sense, all his previous education should be preparation for it but if the examination is to be really worthwhile in scope, the student will need to cover in a general way many areas that have not been included in his previous years of schooling. There should be a clear statement of the ground to be covered and definite suggestions as to which books should be read carefully and which need only be scanned. If it is realistic and carefully developed, this list would make the preparation more meaningful and the examination itself more worth while for the student.

Frequently there is little planning for the orals on the part of faculty members themselves. In some cases the examination is casual and noncomprehensive; on other occasions it propounds questions that the student has had little chance of preparing himself to answer.

Since preparation for the examination should require both course work and independent study—the course work is not expected to cover all the areas on which he will be questioned—the graduate student should begin independent reading and study early. For this reason, a bibliography is useful, as early as the junior year in college.

The student should have an opportunity to make up deficiencies, on a second examination, provided he shows up well generally on the first. The possibility of a second chance would help to reduce the tension and thus encourage students not to postpone this examination unduly.

The graduate council should not only review the reading materials suggested for each of the departments, but provide a bibliography covering the general background of knowledge expected of the student. If such a plan were followed, much of the confusion that now exists about the qualifying examination could be eliminated.

The foreign language requirement is another matter of controversy. Many faculty members, in the social sciences particularly, do not feel the need for foreign language study. In the investigation that Dean Elder made at Harvard he found a large percentage, even at Harvard, who had used little, or none at all, of the required foreign languages in either the course work, general reading, or research for the doctor's degree. In some of the professional schools—such as business administration, engineering, agriculture, and professional education—the foreign language requirement has been waived. In other areas—economics, for example—only one language is required in some institutions, the students being allowed to substitute statistics or some other subject for the second language.[1]

The current language requirements are frequently not up to date. For instance, in some institutions French and German are specified for all students, whereas Russian might be much more useful in certain areas of study, particularly in the scientific and technological ones. Other institutions are liberal in their interpretation of the foreign language requirement, allowing students to present any two foreign languages and not insisting upon high standards. Indeed, too frequently the foreign language examinations are deplored for their lack of satisfactory requirements.

[1] J. P. Elder, *A Criticism of the Graduate School of Arts and Sciences in Harvard University and Radcliffe College.* From those who took the Ph.D. at these institutions between 1950 and 1954, Harvard University Press.

In short, because in many quarters there is no clear conception of the importance of these examinations, no real standards for them have been set, with the result that they are often perfunctory. They do not insure that the student is capable of using the language on which he is examined, as a tool; and, of course, unless he can so use it, the requirement is futile.

The Harvard study showed that many students were seriously delayed in securing their doctorate by having to do special work in languages before being able to pass the examinations. If this is the case at Harvard, how much more true it must be in the less well-established graduate schools.

Obviously this requirement should be met during the college years. If there were early identification of gifted students who are to be encouraged to enter the graduate school, there should be no difficulty in fulfilling the foreign language requirement at least by the end of the first year of graduate work. This would give motivation to the students in foreign language study that is lacking now, and should result in a great saving of time for those who are going on to the doctorate. Indeed, it would seem that one should not be allowed to take a foreign language unless he is required to pursue it long enough to be able to make real use of it. If this were the policy, there would be little reason for the foreign language requirement to be a problem after admission to the doctoral program.

Another matter that is frequently debated is the rationale of the examination on the dissertation. Are students who have completed their course work and produced a satisfactory dissertation rejected for the Ph.D. on account of their showing on the final examination? This should not happen. There can be no justification for such a practice. The Harvard study found a number of former Ph.D. graduates who felt the examination could be eliminated without loss. Many graduate deans incline to the same view.

If there is no substantial reason why the oral on the dissertation should be continued, dispensing with it would save a vast amount of precious faculty time. It could be understood that any faculty member who did not wish to approve the dissertation without asking some questions of the writer, would have the opportunity of doing so. But this would probably not occur often. Conserving faculty time for teaching and research should be given high priority, in view of the shortage of staff and the rapidly expanding enrollments in both the undergraduate and the graduate divisions. In all areas of higher education there should be a constant effort to streamline the program as far as possible in the interest of saving faculty time. The man-hours conserved by a university, which grants one hundred doctorates in a year, in eliminating the dissertation examination would be surprising—probably the equivalent of a full-time professor for a year.

A brief comment on the selection of dissertation topics should be made. Too much time is lost in some universities by students seeking a suitable subject for the dissertation. Some professors, feeling that the student should have enough initiative to find his own topic, give little help. This is unfair to the student. A Ph.D. subject is so specialized that the student should have help in choosing it. He cannot know what is suitable. If the professor would assign two or three topics to the student for investigation and thus allow him some choice in the selection, there would probably not be undue delay, and the investigation would in itself be worth while.

More attention should be paid to dissertation subjects. The unsuitability of some topics and the triviality of others are matters of great concern to thoughtful educators. If they are the criteria by which American higher learning is to be judged, they constitute a sad commentary on it. Some subjects require chiefly an accumulation of detailed facts; others, a report on a piece of mediocre research; and still others, an array of specialized facts and figures to prove a hypothesis that was not worth investigating in the first place. Sometimes there is little science and no trace of philosophy in the subjects on which dissertations are written and for which the Doctor of Philosophy degree is awarded. This should be a matter of deep concern to graduate schools everywhere.

Thus far, in attempting to appraise the soundness of the graduate program, the focus has been largely on the details of practices and procedures that seem ill suited to achieving the best results. In discussing graduate education in the humanities and social sciences, more substantive questions are raised. Is the content of the graduate program in humanistic studies the most appropriate and effective that can be found? Are the methods used in research and in dissertation writing really applicable to this great area of knowledge? Is there a difference between research in the humanities and the social sciences, on the one hand, and in natural science and technology, on the other? These are fundamental questions which deserve attention.

In the natural sciences the bricks and mortar of research are facts, which are used to prove or disprove hypotheses. Their validity rests upon a body of accepted assumptions, facts, and demonstrated principles. In the humanities and the social sciences, ideals and concepts are of primary importance and should be the focus of attention. The range of research should include their origin and development in the history and literature of the past, and their influence upon the outlook in the historical and literary world of the present. The philosophical concepts that have developed in modern times, as well as those inherited from the past, should engage the attention of faculty and graduate students.

The emphasis in current humanistic research appears to be on analysis, just as it is in the natural sciences; but humanistic-social studies should involve synthesis as well. One result of attempting to apply the scientific method rigidly to humanistic-social science research is that it turns out to be research *about* the humanities or social sciences rather than research *in* these fields.

We are living in an age of competing ideologies. Fascism, nazism, communism, and a series of other ideologies alien to Western thought have arisen in this century. A study of the ideas and motivations behind them would throw light on the meaning of the present state of the world. But an examination of the dissertation topics in the field of the humanities reflects little, if any, interest in these important developments. A few researches in some aspects of these subjects are noted—but very few indeed. Thus, it appears that the subject matter of humanities research has generally not been relevant to the modern world. The method of research has frequently not been appropriate, and the results, judged by the reports published by young scholars in the field, are discouraging.

Part 2 *A PROGRAM*

Introduction

The strategic role of graduate education in the American educational system has now been emphasized, and in the light of its importance, its organization, policies, and practices have been examined at length. Defects in many aspects of the program have been pointed out. Occasionally the means of remedying the weaknesses have been suggested, but the main focus of attention has been on defining the issues and indicating their implications.

In most discussions of the subject to date, the conclusion has been either that graduate education, on the whole, is reasonably effective and presents no serious problems, or that it is in a bad state and nothing can be done about it. Those who deplore the present status may make general suggestions designed to improve organization or procedures, policies or practices, but no one has been bold enough to urge such basic and comprehensive reforms as are necessary to modernize the graduate schools, vitalize their operation, increase their output, and improve the quality of their products.

If a university president should undertake to suggest fundamental changes in the structure and authority of the graduate school, which are probably essential to the achievement of optimum results, he would subject himself to the criticism of faculty members who are sensitive about their prerogatives. To make the matter still more difficult, many graduate teachers are satisfied with the status quo and would be inclined to resent drastic changes.

For more than fifty years the organization, methods, and policies of graduate schools have remained essentially unchanged; the policies and practices adopted in the nineteenth century are, in the main, still in force. Why, then, should they be changed? A still more penetrating question might be: How could changes be inaugurated even if they were desirable? The graduate school has no authority to institute them since it has only part-time faculty members.

Effecting these reforms, for which the graduate dean and his faculty will have primary responsibility and authority, will be a major operation. This is probably the reason why no one has proposed them, but it is all the more reason why they should be attempted. The conviction that there must be reform if graduate education is to prosper, prompts the proposal outlined in the following three chapters. This plan will, it is hoped, point the way toward reforms that will enable graduate schools to produce more and better Ph.D. graduates.

In the first chapter, the purpose is to sketch the framework of a new master's degree[1] designed to require a scholarly effort and to produce graduates qualified to do satisfactory college teaching, at least, in the first two years of college. In addition, this program is expected to serve as a means of recruiting for the Ph.D. by choosing only academically talented youth and giving them special preparation for advanced work. It should also serve to insure a more coherent and integrated system of higher education than now exists in most universities.

The twelfth chapter will consider the structure, organization, and authority of the graduate school as well as its substantive policies and practices, with a view to suggesting an approach that would enable it to meet more adequately the present and future needs of graduate education. Reference has been made to the inconsistency of requirements in the several departments represented on the graduate faculty and to the looseness of organization which has resulted in an excessive time lag between the B.A. and the Ph.D. degrees. The new program is designed to resolve these and other issues, which are acute in the area of

---

[1] This is not wholly new, as several institutions have been experimenting with such a program since September 1960.

advanced work beyond the master's degree.

Finally, a chapter summarizing the conclusions and recommendations of the study will review the major problems of graduate education, outline the chief recommendations on the basis of which it is believed they may be solved, and suggest a program designed to modernize the graduate schools, increase their output, and improve their quality.

CHAPTER 11

The Three-Year Master's Degree—
Beginning with the Junior Year

In this chapter it is appropriate to take a brief glance at the status of the first graduate degree as it has developed in American colleges and universities and elsewhere. While fewer than two hundred universities grant the Ph.D. degree, some seven hundred offer one or more master's degree programs. The 1960 edition of *American Universities and Colleges* lists more than 150 kinds of master's degree. Such odd varieties as Master of Criminology (M.Crim.), Master of Television (M.Tv.), Master of Arts in Law and Diplomacy (M.A.L.D.), and Master of Science in Geophysical Engineering (M.S. in Gp. Engr.) are found there. Even more confusing are the Master of Science in Human Relations (M.S. in H.R.) and the Master of Arts in Library Science (M.A. in L.S.)—a science degree in an arts subject, and an arts degree in a science subject.[1]

There is as much variety in the requirements for a given degree, such as the Master of Arts, as there is in the kinds of degree awarded. The M.A. is still occasionally awarded as an honorary degree by such distinguished institutions as Harvard and Yale. As an earned degree, it usually requires one year beyond the B.A., though in some institutions two years are required.

The same inconsistency exists in Britain and other Commonwealth countries. Oxford and Cambridge and some Indian uni-

[1] *American Universities and Colleges* (8th ed.; American Council on Education, 1960).

versities grant the M.A. automatically to the B.A. graduate if he pays fees to his college for three years after graduation. In Scotland the first degree is the M.A., granted for three years of work beyond the secondary school, and the M.A. with honors, after four years, if the program and quality of the student's work warrant it. In short, the master's degree is the center of confusion everywhere so far as requirements for obtaining it are concerned.

In American universities, where the extremes are represented by the honorary degree, on the one hand, and two years of instruction and research beyond the B.A., on the other, there is still further variation. Some institutions require one or more foreign languages, while others require none. Some insist upon a thesis, while others will accept additional course work in lieu of research, and others still will grant the same degree with or without research or thesis. As pointed out earlier, the Master of Arts degree may mean a fifth year of poor undergraduate work, a consolation prize for one who has failed his Ph.D. qualifying examination, a professional degree for the public school teacher, or a scholarly degree given by a university that lays stress upon the first graduate degree. Surely no other area of higher education presents so confused and inconsistent a pattern as that of the master's degree now does. It is unreliable as an index of scholarly achievement. Colleges unable to fill teaching vacancies with Ph.D.'s cannot depend upon the master's degree as qualification for college teaching.

The master's degree here proposed is designed to provide just that. It is unlike any other in the entire category of master's programs. It involves three years of study, which include the upper two years of college. The hope is that the program will not only prepare for college teaching but tie together undergraduate and graduate work in such way as to make all higher education, in the basic fields at least, a consistent, integrated whole. The plan of the degree will be outlined in some detail and will be followed by an appraisal of its possible advantages.

First of all, the new master's degree is not designed for the average college student. It presupposes that membership in the program will be selected from the upper 15 to 20 per cent of the student body, based on scholastic aptitude and achievement. In the nature of the case, this selection must be made not later than the beginning of the third college year. It would be advantageous if the student were tentatively chosen for the program on admission to college.

If only the academically gifted are eligible for admission, the program should not only prepare for teaching in the junior college but also for admission to the Ph.D. qualifying examination and for completion of the work for the Ph.D. in two additional years. With this understanding of the type of student to be chosen and of the general purposes the program is designed to achieve, it is possible to outline the steps involved in setting it up.

Recruiting should begin with high school seniors and continue through the freshman and sophomore years of college. Graduates of junior colleges who had taken the academic course and achieved outstanding records would be another source of supply. Finally, exceptional graduates of four-year colleges who had covered essentially the same ground as that required in the first two years of the three-year program might be eligible to enroll in the third year. Cooperative arrangements might be developed with senior colleges in the region whereby their best graduates would be fully prepared to enter the third year of the three-year program and receive the new master's degree.

Those high school graduates admitted as candidates for the three-year program would be enrolled as "pregraduates," just as those planning to study medicine may enter college as premedical students. If an institution were unwilling to admit a student as a pregraduate on the basis of the high school record, he might be known in his freshman year as a "pregraduate cadet," with the expectation of promotion to pregraduate status in his sophomore year if his record warranted it. The pregraduates should constitute a kind of *honors* group, since all would be highly selected and generally the most capable students on the campus. It should be possible to develop a high *esprit de corps* in the group and through them a higher respect for scholarship on the campus than there would be otherwise.

The pregraduate, at the beginning of his junior year, should have completed the general requirements for the degree in subjects such as English, foreign languages, social science, mathematics, and the natural sciences. This would mean that he could begin concentrating on major and minor subjects at the beginning of his junior year. His scholastic average should place him in the upper 15 to 20 per cent of his class in the first two years of college. Recruits from the freshman and sophomore classes might be chosen whose records in college were superior to those they brought with them from high school. Transfers from other colleges should be permitted to enroll as pregraduates in the sophomore or junior year if their previous college work warranted it.

If junior college graduates should be accepted, it would be important for the university providing the three-year master's degree to have worked out with the junior college the kind of program expected of those who wish to undertake the plan. The same would be true of four-year colleges expecting to transfer students, after awarding the B.A. degree, to this final year of the three-year master's. It would be essential that the program in the upper two years of the four-year college should have developed along the lines prescribed by the university that had developed the three-year program.

What, then, will be expected of the student entering the three-year master's degree plan? As already suggested, the first two years should show marked ability and should be used to complete all of the general requirements for the degree in the institution. With this background, the student would take the regular course work required of others and make at least a "B" average in that work. In addition, he would have special independent reading assignments each of the three years, which would be designed to prepare for the Ph.D. qualifying examination.

In addition to the independent reading assignments, he would be required to write special papers—a semester paper in each of the two semesters of the junior year and a senior essay in the final year of undergraduate work. These papers and essays should be based upon elementary research on some subject assigned by the major professor. In all the writing, beginning with the first semester of the junior year, the student would be required to follow the writing manual that is now usually given students who are writing the master's thesis or the doctor's dissertation. These special assignments of outside reading and writing would introduce to the student the university idea of scholarship beginning with his third year in college. For the able student this not only should be possible but should constitute a challenge of great value to his growth and development. Seminars on the written work of pregraduates, during the first two years of the three-year program, would acquaint him with the methods of scholarly work employed in the graduate schools.

Another requirement of this special degree would be to pass all the foreign language examinations required for the Ph.D. degree. While these must be taken, according to the plan, during the three-year period, it would be highly desirable for this requirement to be met during the last two years of college. A student, who had had only one year of a foreign language before reaching the junior year, would probably need two more years in that language before receiving his bachelor's degree. On the other hand, if he had had two years of foreign language work in the freshman and sophomore classes, he should be able to pass the Ph.D. foreign language examination by taking one additional year.

Since one is expected to be prepared to teach in the junior college on the completion of the three-year master's, some experience in teaching should be provided. Giving a three-hour course for a semester should be the minimum requirement. This may take place in the senior college year or in the final year of the program. Obviously the latter would be preferable, but capable seniors should be able to give acceptable instruction if it is not possible to provide this experience for all in their final year.

The plan of the curriculum is set out in schematic form in Table 5, shown on p. 168.

The faculty organization required for the inauguration and operation of this program is an important consideration. There should be at least two committees: the pregraduate and the graduate committee. A third, the committee on recruitment, will probably be needed, especially in the first few years of the operation of the program. In small institutions three faculty members on each committee might be sufficient, but in larger ones there should probably be five.

The function of the pregraduate committee is to keep in close touch with pregraduates in the same way that premedical committees in good institutions keep in touch with future medical students. Not only should there be personal attention but this committee should also have in mind the ways and means of building up an interest in college teaching as a profession. Its function might include arranging meetings for the pregraduate group to hear distinguished speakers on some phase of college and university work, the role of the college and university professor in modern society, or on other topics designed to develop an appreciation of the importance of teaching as a profession.

On the pregraduate faculty committee there should be a majority from the undergraduate faculty with at least one from the graduate school; and on the graduate committee, a majority from the graduate faculty.

If the pregraduate committee is charged with recruiting, which would involve visiting the high schools, junior colleges, and four-year colleges in the area, it would be necessary to provide considerable released time for this and its other functions, particularly during the first few years of the program.

The graduate committee would have a different kind of function. It would be responsible for working with the heads of the various departments to develop reading lists for the use of the

TABLE 5

EDUCATED BEYOND THE HIGH SCHOOL FOR THE GIFTED*

This sketch is designed to assist the reader in visualizing the entire post-high school program for the gifted student and in seeing the relation of the three-year master's scheme to the preceding two years and to the final two years leading to the doctorate.

1st. Year	2nd. Year	3rd. Year	4th. Year	5th. Year	6th. Year	7th. Year
Requirements of all students taking bachelor's degree to be completed in first two years		Three-Year Master's Degree Concentration and beginning specialization foreign languages and electives				
In Humanities Social Sciences Natural Sciences Mathematics and Foreign Languages		Research Semester Papers	Research Senior Essay	Research Master's Thesis	Research and Specialization	Research and Writing of the Dissertation
		Majors, Minors, Foreign Languages and Electives				
Pre-graduate Cadet (probationary status)		Pre-graduate		Honors Master's Degree		
		Independent reading from list provided by the faculty in preparation for the Ph.D. qualifying examinations and passing foreign language examinations for doctor's degree.			Ph.D. qualifying examinations— 1st semester	
				3 semester hours of teaching M.Phil.,	Course work required by the graduate faculty	Examination on the dissertation
			B.A. or B.S.		M.A. or M.S.	Ph.D. (or D. Phil.)

three-year master's students. Since their independent reading is to be designed as general preparation for the Ph.D. qualifying examination, it would be necessary for this committee, with the help of the department heads, to define more clearly the purposes, the scope, and the type of preparation needed for this examination.

Separate reading lists should be prepared for each of the three years, the junior, senior, and first year of graduate work. This would require not only thinking through the material to be covered but determining its arrangement by years, so that the outside reading would be best suited to the intellectual growth of the students. The interest of a faculty committee in the progress of students in their independent reading and writing assignments should be a source of real stimulation and motivation.

This committee should also probably take the major responsibility for working with the four-year colleges in the area, helping them so to arrange their requirements in the upper two years that they will fit the student for admission to the three-years master's program in the university.

Another responsibility of the graduate committee would be to see that all enrollees in the program complete their foreign language examinations within the three-year period.

Still other functions of the graduate committee might be to check on the independent reading being done by the students and on the quality of written work required of the juniors and seniors. It might be responsible for arranging occasional seminars on the written work to insure that the papers and essays are more than perfunctory exercises.

If the committee is to fulfill these several functions adequately, the members will require considerable released time, particularly during the first few years.

Under the plan no special classes are required for students in the three-year program—only special independent reading and writing assignments. The junior and senior students in the program will take the same courses as other juniors and seniors. A student will choose a major and minors in conference with the department head, as they are chosen by all other students. The averages for all students in the three-year program will, however, be "B" or above. Anyone who is barely making a "B" average shall be the object of special consideration by the pregraduate faculty committee. The grade average and the reading and writing requirements will be all that will distinguish the student in the special program from his classmates. The successful student in the program will have to develop habits of independent study which are not required of the other students.

Not all the special requirements have to be met during term time. Some of them may be fulfilled during summer vacations. The reading assignments might be largely done in vacation time. Written work could also be undertaken then. Even the foreign language examinations could be prepared for during the summers. It is desirable that under such a plan each year's reading assignment should be completed within the twelve-month period after the list is presented to the student. For example, the list presented to a junior in September should be completed by the following September.

The foreign language requirement should also receive early attention. The student should find out early in his junior year precisely what the graduate faculty committee expects of him by way of preparation for the examination, and undertake to begin that preparation in the first year of the program.

The independent reading and study plan, so essential to the success of the program, will require the special attention of students and faculty. American students are not usually experienced in independent study. They will need help in understanding what it means and how to carry it out. Definite reading habits, over and above preparation for class work, should be developed. The faculty committees should be conscious of this problem and devise ways and means of solving it. Each faculty will know how best to meet this issue on its campus.

The development of sound independent reading habits is probably the most essential single task the student will have in this program. The next most difficult problem he will have is that of becoming accustomed to writing research papers. American students in high school and college have far too little experience in handling abstract ideas and in written expression. Special attention in this program should be given to the research papers. If properly organized, the subjects of the semester papers in the junior year might be in the nature of a report on some part of the outside reading required in that year.

This plan would not only stimulate the student's reading but help him retain the knowledge acquired through that reading. In that way both the reading and the writing programs would be strengthened. The major professor, who would presumably assign topics for the research papers, should have full knowledge of the plans of the graduate committee for the independent reading program.

Not only in the papers required in the junior year but in the senior essay and in the master's thesis, it is conceivable that the reading assignments could provide the basic source material. This would add to the effectiveness of the program by linking the research and writing with the independent reading requirements.

The students should understand early in their careers as pregraduates that if they do not complete their work during the nine-month academic year, they will be expected to attend summer school. In a plan of this kind it is essential that one year's requirements are completed before the next year is begun. Summer school may be particularly important for those who find difficulty in meeting the language requirements. Special summer sessions, giving intensive language instruction, could be set up in order to insure that no student would complete the program without having passed the language examinations. Likewise, if a student got behind in his outside reading, he would be expected to attend a summer session if necessary to complete it.

With this background in mind—the nature of the faculty organization, the requirements of the students in the three-year

master's program, and the means of insuring that these requirements are met—let us take a look at the advantages of this
special three-year program to the graduate school and to the
students involved.

The first great advantage is the provision it makes for early
identification of talented students. As already suggested, this
should begin with high school seniors. Where a successful
three-year master's program is in operation, it might be possible
to stimulate the high schools in the area to vie with each other
over the number of their graduates accepted in the pregraduate
program. Such rivalry should result in an upgrading of the work
of the secondary schools.

A second advantage would be the extra opportunities for
learning, which the superior student would have under this
program. Too frequently the able students take the same course
with the same requirements as the weakest students. When this
happens, the superior student lacks adequate challenge and is
likely to develop bad study habits. He fails to stretch his mind
or to learn to make a real effort. Members of a pregraduate
group would be challenged early to put forth effort, since the
requirements would be rigorous, and each pregraduate would
be in competition with able classmates. Pregraduate status
would give him some prestige among his fellow students, for
in a real sense he would be recognized as an honors student.
From the beginning, as much, or more, prestige should be
attached to being a pregraduate as to being a premedical student.
There is little doubt that in time the pregraduate group would
be recognized by faculty and students alike as the most important and influential of student organizations.

A third advantage is that such a program would assist greatly
in the articulation of undergraduate and graduate work. At the
present time there is no real meshing of undergraduate with
graduate studies. One completes his Bachelor of Arts degree
with little notion of the difference between undergraduate and
graduate work. The result is that if he chooses to go into a bona
fide master's degree program, he finds himself at a loss to

know how to go about the work expected of him as a graduate student. This should not be true, particularly of able students. They should have some acquaintance with the university idea of scholarship before completing their undergraduate work. This acquaintance, the three-year master's program is designed to provide.

Reference has been made to the value the high schools might derive from the presence in their area of a university with a three-year master's program. This program should also encourage scholarship in the junior colleges, as it is well suited to the needs of their graduates. A packaged program, three years in length, which would prepare the junior college student for teaching in his alma mater or in the first two years of some four-year college, should have wide appeal, and the requirements of the upper two years of the program would stimulate him to greater effort.

The program would help build up standards not only in the junior college but in the cooperating four-year college also. The list of books for outside reading given to the university juniors and seniors could be provided the juniors and seniors in the four-year cooperating colleges. This would be necessary in order to prepare the college graduate for entering the three-year program in its last year. Written work would also be required. This should give the abler four-year college students a new outlook and motivation as well as a stronger program.

During the next decade many college teachers will have less than Ph.D. training. At present no master's degree program is designed to qualify graduates for college teaching. Relatively few M.A. graduates are qualified for the task. An urgent need exists for a new kind of program that prepares for college teaching. The three-year master's with its special requirements, its rigorous training, and its emphasis on college teaching as a goal, should be the answer. The acute need for M.A.'s qualified for college teaching should make a strong appeal in recruiting students. It should be noted, however, that master's degree holders under the three-year plan will also be in great demand by government, business, and industry, all of which now require more than a bachelor's degree for many positions. The master's graduate under the program here outlined would probably be in as great demand from government, business and industry as from the colleges and universities. In short, the program should appeal to as many prospective government, commercial and industrial employees as to prospective teachers. This means that not one but four fields would be open to the three-year master's graduate.

The program has other advantages than merely preparing for professional opportunities. It should assist in developing habits of reading and independent study, which too few college graduates acquire. Their failure to acquire such habits is perhaps because they are not expected to. This plan, by requiring independent work beyond that necessary for regular classes attended, would contribute to the development of intellectual interests and initiative.

Another advantage of this program is its provision for attracting able students into college teaching as a profession. The faculties of colleges and universities have tended to discount the profession and, therefore, to discourage students from entering it. This accounts, in part, for the present shortage of teachers. It is unjustified and, at the same time, damaging. If college and university professors fail to encourage students with ability to follow in their footsteps, the future of higher education is dim. Both the pregraduate and graduate committees, working closely with an able group of students, who are enrolled in a program designed to train for college teaching, would have a natural context within which to talk with the students about their future and informally to acquaint them with the needs and opportunities of the profession of college teaching.

The liberal arts students who have not decided on a profession, have generally had limited contacts with their teachers and students, especially the able students. In contrast, the premedical committees have had a profound influence on students planning to enter medicine and, in the long run, on the medical profession itself. To a lesser extent perhaps, the faculties working with pre-law and prenursing students have had the same effect. But those who are uncertain about their choice of a career or think they might later enter graduate school, have no such natural contacts with the faculty. The proposed program provides for the ablest of that group at least, giving the faculty an excellent opportunity to present the case for the profession of college teaching.

This plan likewise provides an effective means of recruiting for the Ph.D. degree. In time, it is conceivable that the three-year master's degree might become the gateway to the qualifying examination and to work for the Ph.D. It would have the effects of identifying able students early and of providing a special program for them—and a program pointed in the direction of the doctorate. This would reduce enormously the attrition rate in the graduate school and shorten the gap between the B.A. and the Ph.D. Indeed, it should be possible for 90 per cent of the three-year master's degree holders to achieve the doctorate in two more years.

Undoubtedly one of the great needs in graduate education, in view of the shortage of Ph.D.'s, is some means of producing more and better Ph.D. graduates. This cannot take place unless the colleges do more than merely qualify their students by giving the bachelor's degree. They must prepare them by providing them early with some knowledge of the university idea of scholarship, some experience in independent study, and some practice in writing reports on their reading and research. With such preparation an able student should be as sure of obtaining the Ph.D. two years after getting his master's as the medical student is of receiving the M.D. four years after his enrollment in medical school. This would reduce the waste "of student energy, hope and money and of faculty time and effort," but, more than that, it should provide better graduates because they would be prepared for advanced graduate work before entering upon the Ph.D. program.

If some such plan as that sketched above were developed, there is little doubt that the graduate schools would be able to produce more and better Ph.D.'s and at the same time, through the guidance and stimulation of secondary schools, junior colleges, and four-year colleges, strengthen the entire program of higher education substantially.

Another special advantage of the program should be its appeal to women to enter college teaching. Most women students hesitate to undertake three years or more of graduate work in pursuit of the Ph.D. degree, but might easily be persuaded to commit themselves to one year beyond the bachelor's degree, particularly if it qualified them for college teaching.

A study conducted by the Research Division of the N.E.A. in 1958 revealed that 87.2 per cent of all public elementary teachers, 53.7 per cent of high school teachers, and 21.8 per cent of college and university teachers are women. If the fields of home economics, library science, and women's physical and health education were excluded, 90 per cent of the total college and university staff would be men, according to the study's findings. The same study found also that 79.2 per cent of the institutions investigated were willing to employ more women in one or more fields. For example, ninety-seven institutions expressed a willingness to employ more women in English; ninety-two wanted more in social science; ninety-one in mathematics; sixty-seven in education; etc.[2]

The need for attracting more able women into college teaching is obvious; the willingness of institutions to employ them has been ascertained; the ingredient lacking is a program designed to prepare them for the task. The three-year master's degree provides that program. Any plan that could tap the large reservoir of talented women students and prepare them adequately for college teaching would make a substantial contribution toward the solution of the teacher shortage.

What should be the title of such a degree? Some suggest that it should be a simple Master of Arts, or of Science; others say an Honors degree or a Master of Philosophy. The variety of M.A.'s

[2] *Research Report* ("Higher Education Series," 1959-R10 [Washington, D.C.: N.E.A. Research Division, 1959]). *Teacher Supply and Demand in Universities, Colleges, and Junior Colleges, 1957-58 and 1958-59.*

now offered discourages the use of this title without something to distinguish it from the others.

The degree of Master of Philosophy, with the abbreviation M.Phil., would be distinctive. It would duplicate no degree now given in the United States. There is a Master of Philosophy degree, but it is not common and, its abbreviation is Ph.M. If the program proves successful and becomes widespread, it is possible that the degree, whatever its designation, would have unique prestige among the master's degrees given. This could happen only if the students were superior; if the requirements for admission were truly rigorous; and if the demands made of students were stiff but well planned. If the degree has no designation other than a Master of Arts, there may be confusion which would delay its optimum development.

CHAPTER 12

The Graduate School and the Doctor's Degree

The three-year master's program outlined in the preceding chapter is designed to achieve three major objectives: (1) to prepare able students for teaching in junior colleges or in the first two years of a four-year college; (2) to give the basic education and experience required of those who may wish to proceed to the doctorate; and (3) to provide for an arrangement of courses and experiences that will meld the undergraduate and graduate programs in such way as to produce a logical, coherent, and integrated program of basic higher education extending from high school graduation to the Doctor of Philosophy degree.

It is concerned primarily with the basic studies, though it may be extended to include such undergraduate professional schools as engineering and business education. It is designed to cater primarily to the needs of the ablest students, not to those of the average or below average groups, on the theory that graduate students should come, in the main, from the upper 20 per cent of the undergraduate student body. Through the plans suggested for cooperation with the two-year and four-year colleges in the admission of transfers from them, this program has an opportunity to influence the quality of work done as far as the master's degree in all institutions of higher learning in the field of the basic studies. By providing special preparation for Ph.D. work, it should also affect indirectly the quality of the most advanced graduate studies.

However successful the three-year master's program may be, its effectiveness as a method of recruiting for the doctor's degree may be lost unless the graduate school solves some of its problems. These have been detailed in Chapter 9 and need not be repeated. Confusion, lack of consistency, high attrition rate, the lag between the B.A. and the Ph.D., and lack of responsibility and authority of the graduate faculty as an organized segment of the university are among the more basic issues.

More than one hundred different kinds of master's and sixty-eight varieties of doctorates illustrate the extent to which the field of knowledge has been fragmented. Professional doctorates are usually outside the jurisdiction of the graduate school, and as a result there is little control over their expansion in numbers or over the standards maintained. Since the doctorate is a coveted degree in any field and since all professional groups seek university affiliation for their training programs, there seems to be no end to the proliferation of doctor's degrees.

Each university should study this problem with a view to insuring that its standards are maintained, that some restraint is exercised in the multiplication of graduate degrees, and that it does not fall into the error of providing instruction and research in subjects inappropriate to its mission. Even in the Ph.D. programs of well-established graduate schools the appropriateness of the areas of research and instruction might well be re-examined.

The lack of consistency among departments in the same university in their requirements for graduate degrees, including the doctorate, is inexcusable. When a graduate student in one department requires normally one or two years more for the doctorate than one enrolled in another department, the effect is to discredit the university and its graduate school. Indeed, under the present organization there is no way to enforce a consistent policy, since each department may set its own standards within limits, and, in some important decisions, an individual professor may prevent a student from receiving his degree by declining to approve his dissertation. In short, there are no systematic controls over graduate faculty members such as there are in colleges and professional schools. This accounts for the inconsistent practices and other weaknesses in the graduate school.

The attrition rate in graduate schools is a most puzzling phenomenon. The absence of systematic and consistent controls may be a partial explanation. The lack of preparation for graduate work in the college may also be partially responsible. Certainly better recruitment and more effective admission policies and methods would help to eliminate the great waste of time, hope, and money of students and the energy of faculty members involved in this process. But something more than all these improvements may be required. Perhaps it is the tone of the graduate school that is at fault—the preoccupation of members of the staff, their indifference to the student, the uncertainties with respect to the program, thesis, or dissertation topic, the foreign language requirement, qualifying examination, courses that should be taken, etc.

The operation of the graduate school is often unbusinesslike and unimpressive to the entering student. In that atmosphere the newcomer tends to drift and, in time, to become discouraged. The entire operation needs to be tightened up. More rigorous demands, more clearly defined procedures, more definite and explicit instruction as to expectations should replace the usual uncertainties that surround the novice. In short, what is needed is a more efficient operation.

Closely related to attrition is the excessive time required for achieving the Ph.D. The same conditions that result in permanent drop-outs apply to those who are not sufficiently challenged to stay and complete work for the degree. Here again, indifference of the faculty and uncertainty as to the length of time required produce discouragement. Shortage of funds also plays its part, but this could be overcome more easily if the student could be given some assurance as to how long it would take to finish the work required for the degree.

What is the remedy for these shortcomings? The only answer that seems to make sense is an organization of the graduate school that insures that some group of faculty members shall have as their primary obligation the development of a sound and efficient program of graduate education and the authority necessary to put it into effect. It is inconceivable that anything short of this can handle effectively the three hundred thousand graduate students now thronging our universities and double and treble this number who will be knocking at the doors of the graduate schools in the next ten to fifteen years.

Unless some such step is taken, the present confusion in graduate education will be more confounded. The number of departments announcing doctoral programs is increasing each year; the number of institutions moving into advanced graduate work is growing rapidly; and there is no agency authorized to check on the validity of new programs, the quality of the work being done, or the standards prevailing in the new institutions. In short, we have this anomalous situation: the most strategic —and potentially, if not actually, the most influential—division of higher education is unorganized at all levels—local, state, regional, and national. This obtains because under the present organization no faculty or administrative group has a primary obligation for graduate education or authority to effect changes in the present program, however much they may be needed.

If there were local autonomy in graduate education, the several autonomous groups could organize for effective action to solve its manifold problems and to improve the program generally. Without more responsibility and authority at the local level, there can be no effective action at any other level. In other words, a group of units, each of which has no primary responsibility or authority, can be no more effective than its constituent elements. This doubtless accounts for the fact that there is no comprehensive national organization of graduate schools concerned with the improvement of graduate education.

In addition to the specific internal problems of graduate education, there are broad areas of concern which should be the object of continuous study by some responsible group. They are: (1) the nature of research and graduate instruction in the humanities and social sciences; (2) the relation of the graduate school to the college; (3) the problem of preparing an adequate number of qualified college and university teachers; and (4) the means of increasing the number and improving the quality of scientists to man the classrooms and laboratories of the colleges and universities and to supply the needs of government, business, and industry. Obviously these are all in the areas for which the graduate school must take responsibility. They cannot be dealt with adequately by a part-time faculty. They are, indeed, central problems in American higher education.

Dissatisfaction with instruction and research in the humanistic-social studies field has been characteristic of the past fifty years. This has been particularly true since the end of World War II, when science and technology began to assume new importance in the university. There are two aspects of the problem: (1) the de-emphasis on all subjects not related to the natural sciences and technology, and (2) discontent with graduate work, particularly in the humanities.

The humanities (language, literature, history, and philosophy) constituted the core of the university curriculum for several hundred years before science and technology were recognized as worthy subjects of research and study. Less than a century, however, after science and technology were grudgingly accorded a place in the program of higher education, they began to claim the lion's share of the budget, and the ablest young men and women began to be attracted by them, with the result that humanistic-social studies were relegated to a secondary position in the scheme of higher education.

Certain basic university traditions are threatened by these revolutionary changes. Methods of instruction have undergone basic changes; the laboratory of the market place has largely replaced the ivory tower; inductive empirical investigation has replaced deductive logic; and the goals of university education have shifted from emphasis on individual development to emphasis on producing trained manpower in response to society's needs. These fundamental departures from tradition have re-

sulted in specialization, the fragmentation of knowledge, focusing on minor problems instead of major issues, and substituting
pursuit of knowledge for the pursuit of truth as the basic goal of
university education. The significance of these shifts has largely
escaped notice under the pressure of an expanding science and
technology. The graduate faculties, which produce the college
teaching personnel, determine the direction of change in higher
education but, because of their concentration on specialized
research, their part-time status, and their lack of concern about
what is happening in the colleges, have apparently been unaware
of their responsibility for maintaining the intellectual traditions
so essential to sound university education.

This has been one of the factors in the decline of the liberal
arts, which has been so eloquently deplored by Mr. McGrath.
Graduate education, built around the method employed in
natural science research, has stressed a different approach to
learning from that of the traditional college. It has emphasized
objectivity, established principles, demonstrated facts. The
scientific method has no place for *values* which involve subjective judgments. Its approach is analytical; synthesis is rarely
required. Liberal education, on the other hand, must be concerned with basic concepts and ideals.

More important than the acquisition of facts is the development of a sense of values. Provision must be made in college
for education in values. This may be largely a by-product of the
educational process, but it requires more than mere factual
instruction. It must involve the development of judgments,
wrestling with the issues of good and evil, right and wrong,
justice and injustice, etc. Graduate work as it is now conducted
does little to train one for instruction of this type.

This complaint is raised in connection not with the teaching
of science but only with the humanities and social sciences. Graduate school faculties have not concerned themselves sufficiently
with this problem. In fact, they have been inclined to say that
their role is to develop scholars and scientists, not teachers. But
this is untenable. More than one half the Ph.D.'s go into edu-

cational work, and most of them teach. No other agency is qualified to train college and university teachers. The graduate schools cannot escape responsibility for this task, and yet one rarely, if ever, hears of a graduate school appointing a faculty committee to study ways and means of providing a better teacher preparation program.

The graduate school should recognize its responsibility for college teacher preparation and gird for action in this area. Faculty study of the problems involved, including the basic difference that exists now between graduate and liberal education, should result in a greatly improved program of higher education. Whether by design or default, the graduate schools determine the destiny of the college, since all college teachers are the products of these schools. Thus, the failure of the college is to be counted a failure of the graduate school. By the same token, the success of the college will be a tribute to the graduate school. The doctrine that the prime object of graduate education is scholarship and that teacher preparation is not its responsibility, is not only false but dangerous.

This statement refers to whether the whole scheme of education provided in the graduate schools is sound and designed to give the proper preparation for teachers of college youth. There is no problem in higher education more fundamental to the future of American educational progress than this, and it is the graduate faculty that has responsibility for seeking its solution. It will require the same painstaking study and experimentation as the research problem that engages the attention of the scholar or the scientist.

As suggested earlier, the attempt to apply the scientific method literally to the humanistic-social studies field has been responsible for much confusion, frustration, and ineffectiveness, because the development of the natural sciences is far advanced over that of the humanities and the social sciences.

The primary need in the humanistic-social science areas of the curriculum is for a study of the significant ideas and ideals upon which our culture rests. As suggested in chapters 5 and

6, if graduate education and research should concentrate upon identifying and clarifying the basic tenets underlying Western culture, it would have a chance of revitalizing liberal studies, of resolving the problem of college teacher preparation in graduate schools, and of meshing undergraduate and graduate studies in these two broad fields of knowledge.

In an ideological age such as ours, an understanding of the faith by which we live is surely as important as the technology by which we hope to defend it. In the long run the strength of that faith may be a greater bulwark against defeat than superior science and technology. Some knowledge of the origin, development, and influence of the ideas and ideals that are the dynamic elements in our society, is essential to an appreciation of our heritage. The concepts of human dignity, inalienable rights, social justice, equality of opportunity, the brotherhood of man, the fatherhood of God, social responsibility, the rights of man, and many others are central to our modes of thought and way of life. Each of them has an origin, and each finds expression in the history, literature, and philosophy of our culture. To trace their origin, development, and influence would comprehend the entire spectrum of liberal education, of the basic aspects of the higher learning.

If these should be the focus of basic graduate education in the humanities and social studies, the Ph.D. holder in language, literature, history, or philosophy would be prepared to give fundamental instruction. By orienting the undergraduate to this conception of liberal education, one could hope to produce a new attitude toward liberal learning, a new motivation and, hence, a new interest in it. It might be, thus, possible to revive the liberal arts in university education and restore them to their original central position.

Such an approach would require more than a simple analysis of basic concepts; it would require also a synthesis of the elements of each to arrive at an understanding of the impact of the concept as a whole. Similarly, such an approach would involve more than simple facts. In an effort to comprehend the influence of a given concept on society, one would have to compare, contrast, and make judgments. This would necessitate constant evaluation and appraisal. In other words, it would call not only for facts but for value judgments.

The chief complaint registered against graduate schools, so far as their teacher preparation function is concerned, is related to the humanities and social sciences. There is also criticism of science instruction in the colleges. There is little if any complaint about the teaching of science majors, but there is concern about the instruction in science of non-science majors. Many experiments have been conducted in pursuit of a more appropriate and effective method of helping non-science students understand science and the scientific method, the most notable of which, described earlier, was conducted by President Conant of Harvard.

The series of changes suggested for the three broad fields of knowledge cannot be effected easily or speedily. Much research and experimentation would be required over a period of years before such a program could be inaugurated. Neither these nor any other significant changes can be effected under the present organization of graduate schools.

It may be relevant at this point to submit a series of statements indicating the present deep discontent with the organization and results of graduate education as now conducted in American universities.

Dean Gordon Whaley, of the University of Texas, in a recent address, said: "It is my considered opinion that something better than 90 percent of the functions ordinarily performed by most of the deans of our graduate schools represent an utter waste of the dean's time, if he is any good at all, and add up to a far more negative than positive impact upon what is desirable in graduate education."[1]

Former Dean Hugh Taylor of Princeton, in speaking of graduate education, said: "One central problem is that of attrition." In the highly selective Graduate School of Princeton "only

[1] Address by Dean Gordon Whaley, University of Texas, 1960.

about three-fifths of the students admitted as Ph.D. candidates actually succeed in obtaining the degree." In commenting on the report of the Dean of the Graduate Faculties at Columbia, he had this further to say: "But the waste remains appalling— nearly 50 percent of the entrants of 1948 still had no degree in 1956. It is waste on both sides—of student energy, hope and money, and of faculty time and effort. This failure is as clear from the statistics as it is from simple reflection on common experience."[2]

Another facet of the problem was stressed by Dr. John E. Horner of Hanover College, who pointed out that the catalogue announcements of seventy-five institutions studied revealed a total of 14,732 courses open to graduate students. Of these, some 62 per cent were mixed courses, while approximately 5,600 were open only to graduate students.[3] This is revealing in light of the facts brought out by Bernard Berelson that in the period from 1911 to 1920 over 90 per cent of the doctorates were conferred in the traditional arts and sciences, while since World War II only about two thirds were conferred in the academic disciplines.

The failure of graduate schools to meet more than one third of the demand for Ph.D. graduates has been confirmed by several recent studies. Despite this urgent need, Dean Elder of Harvard pointed out in 1958 that often the graduate faculty makes two errors. First, it is frequently hazy about what is demanded for a good performance in the general examinations, with the result that the "nervously bewildered student either overprepares or, wandering about in academic disorder, does not prepare as well as he might. Straight, practical advice from a professor could save much waste of time and emotion here." In the second place, in some fields "the amount of the material upon which the candidate may be examined is preposterously large."[4]

Dean Nichols of the University of Pennsylvania pointed out

[2] Sir Hugh Taylor, *Graduate Education at Princeton,* 1945 to 1958.
[3] John E. Horner, "A Dangerous Trend in Graduate Education," *The Journal of Higher Education,* XXX, No. 3 (March 1959), pp. 167-8.
[4] J. P. Elder, *A Criticism of the Graduate School of Arts and Sciences in Harvard University and Radcliffe College,* Harvard Press, p. 22.

that the graduate dean "can, in certain instances, be described as little more than a registrar and student counselor" because he has "little to do with recruiting or advancing faculty," "no direct influence on maintaining graduate-faculty quality," and "yet he and his part-time associates are responsible for the highest quality of university instruction and for the carrying out of some of the most difficult objectives of higher education."[5]

Dean Stewart of the University of California, calling attention to "the dangers of failure to keep pace with a changing society and of debasement of the quality of graduate education," pointed out that less uniformity of organization "exists among graduate schools than among colleges" and warned that "if the differences become too great, advanced degrees will ultimately lose all meaning."[6]

The importance attached to graduate education and research is graphically illustrated by the growth of graduate school enrollments from 106,119 in 1940 to 305,000 in 1960. Even more impressive is the growth in Federal support from $15,000,000.00 in 1940 to $440,000,000.00 in 1959. The threefold increase in graduate students and the thirtyfold increase in government support in twenty years represent the startling expansion of the graduate education enterprise in the United States but, according to the statements of leading graduate school deans quoted above, the graduate school organization has not been adequate.

The graduate school faculty is made up of a group of indiivduals, each of whom is an autonomous unit. The graduate dean cannot exercise effective control. As Dean Nichols pointed out:

In terms of the usual connotation of the word, he is not a dean at all. He has a faculty to be sure, but he does not recruit it, pay it or promote it. He cannot effectively either reward or admonish it. He cannot deal effectively with department heads in any direct face-to-face relationship in any realistic atmosphere of academic negotiation. The department heads

[5] Roy F. Nichols, "The Ambiguous Position of the Graduate-School Dean," *The Journal of Higher Education*, XXX, No. 3 (March 1959), p. 125.
[6] *The Journal of Higher Education*, XXX, No. 3 (March 1959), pp. 136-7.

know, and he knows, that they must look to other deans for new appointments, promotions, increases in salary; they must negotiate elsewhere than in his office.[7]

This describes the disorganization and confusion that prevail in that segment of higher education which has the greatest responsibility and opportunity of all. There is no doubt that at the present time the graduate school occupies the most strategic and fateful role of any division of the university. For that reason, reorganization of the graduate schools in such way as to enable them to meet their responsibilities is a primary and imperative need of American higher education.

Sir Hugh Taylor, former dean of the Graduate School at Princeton, suggests:

What is needed is an understanding appreciation by the president of the importance of the dean of the graduate school in the whole educational hierarchy—and a public expression by the president to his faculty of his desire for improvement in graduate studies and his support of and confidence in the dean of the graduate school to secure these ends.[*]

He would oppose changing the status of the dean or his faculty, though he says: "I think that the reorganization and strengthening of graduate schools is the primary problem."[8] Perhaps if his experience had been in a large state university, his conclusions would have been different. In a multipurpose university with twenty thousand students and fifteen instructional divisions, it is extremely doubtful that one could insure the priority, prestige, and effectiveness of a graduate program and its dean on such an informal basis.

I am aware of the objections that have been raised: (1) that to set up a graduate faculty with a budget would require a "major revolution" in universities; (2) that "it would further fragmentize faculties"; (3) that "it would probably set off an elite which would become as isolated and insulated as some of the professional faculties"; and (4) that "it would set up a com-

[7] Nichols, *loc. cit.*, pp. 124-5.
[*] Letter to the author.
[8] Taylor, *op. cit.*

peting vested interest." Let us examine each of these complaints realistically.

If it would require a major revolution to provide the dean of the most important division of the university with a faculty and a budget, there could be no clearer proof that a revolution is necessary. It means simply that universities are afflicted with a virulent case of conservatism, which requires drastic action. The mounting unmet needs of graduate education are further evidence of the need for unprecedented measures.

The argument that to place the dean of the graduate school on the same footing as other deans would "further fragmentize faculties" carries little weight. If the graduate faculties had been stronger in the past, they might have been able to prevent the worst form of fragmentation known to higher education—the establishment of graduate divisions of professional schools, which award their own degrees. The organization of graduate schools must be strengthened in order to prevent wholesale fragmentation in graduate education. A strong graduate school should be able so to reorganize its offerings as to eliminate much of the fragmentation that now exists.

The fear that a graduate faculty set up like other faculties might create an elite group appears to be largely unfounded. All full-time graduate faculty members should be required to teach at least one semester of an undergraduate course each year. At the same time a substantial proportion of the graduate course work and student supervision should be conducted by undergraduate and professional teaching staffs co-opted by the graduate dean for this work. Such an ararngement should eliminate not only the possibility of an isolated elite but also the danger of such a faculty's becoming a "competing vested interest."

In the light of all the facts—the desperate need for more and better graduate education, the current waste of time and energy of faculty and students, the recognized inefficiences of the present system, the expanding need in the future, and the overwhelming importance of graduate education to the educational system and to the governmental, business, and industrial interests of the country—I can see no alternative to such re-organization of the graduate schools as will make them effective administrative as well as educational divisions. Such a reform seems to me the essential first step in the improvement of graduate education. If taken, it should inspire new confidence, new interest, and new support.

The basic changes needed in graduate education will not be achieved, however, unless the efforts to achieve them receive widespread support. All higher education agencies and associations have a stake in the matter—the American Association of Universities, the American Council on Education, the American Association of Colleges, etc. But more than the interest and support of educators will be needed. Substantial financial aid will be required, if changes are to be effected in time to meet expanding needs. The chances of financial backing appear to be good. Business, industry, and government all have a stake in the success of graduate education. All are clamoring for Ph.D.'s, well-trained men and women, not simply in mathematics and the natural sciences but also in the humanities and the social sciences. The vast sums of money industry is investing in advanced training programs within its own organizations indicate its concern, and the National Defense Education Act is clear evidence of the government's interest.

An emerging demand on universities, in the field of graduate instruction and research, is that of providing for post-doctoral students. An increasing number of post-doctoral fellowships are being awarded annually. This rapid growth of advanced students since 1950 prompted one president to write: "Post-doctoral training will, in a few years, be of major magnitude in many universities. This is inevitable in the light of the growing complexity of knowledge, and the need in universities, industries, and government for scholars trained to high creative levels."[9]

This phase of university responsibility has grown so rapidly that no uniformity in the handling of post-doctoral fellows has

[9] Statement of Milton S. Eisenhower in response to questionnaire from the author.

been developed. In some institutions charges are made for certain types of post-doctoral work; in others, there are none. Some agencies, making grants to individuals for post-doctoral research and study, provide funds to the universities where the student does his work; in other cases the universities bear the total cost of providing space and materials for the post-doctoral student.

The demand is of recent origin. Ten years ago it was so small as to be negligible, but in 1960-61 the number of post-doctoral students in a single institution was about 500 and in others more than 350.[10] The expansion of knowledge, the explosion of interest in research on the part of the government, business and industry, and the demand for greater and greater specialization mean that a vast increase of post-doctoral students may be expected within the decade. It is, therefore, of the greatest importance that planning should be under way to meet this increase.

Obviously it is the graduate schools that must do the planning if the universities are to meet this challenge, but under the present organization these schools are not in a position to undertake it. The post-doctoral demand is a good illustration of the expanding responsibilities of graduate education, which make planning for the future imperative. Such planning will require studies of various kinds, which cannot be appropriately developed by any agency of the university except the graduate school.

But a part-time staff could not be expected to devote the required time and energy to such studies. The graduate dean has no funds available for their support, even if the faculty had time to plan them. Moreover, the history and the traditions of the graduate school, as well as its policies and practices, do not suggest planning for the future as one of its functions. No national study of graduate education needs, initiated by graduate schools, has been undertaken.

Medical schools, law schools, engineering schools, architectural schools, nursing schools, theological schools, four-year colleges, and junior colleges have been studied and restudied.

---

[10] Data secured from questionnaire sent to university presidents.

Reports of these studies involve a vast literature, and the basic reforms that have resulted from them constitute some of the most significant chapters in the history of university education. While studies of graduate education have been made, apparently none has been sponsored by the graduate schools, and no significant changes have resulted from studies made by individuals. The reason for this situation inheres in the nature of the graduate school organization. Until this is modified there is little, if any, hope for significant planning or for important changes in graduate school operations or procedures. This reinforces the view that the reorganization of graduate schools is imperative if the demands of the future are to be met.

The reorganization proposed is not radical. It involves placing the graduate school in the same position as all other divisions of the university by providing a budget and giving to the dean of the school the same sort of authority that the deans of other schools and colleges have.

Under such a plan the faculty members would have, as a central responsibility, the study and improvement of graduate education. As already suggested, each should give at least one undergraduate course, and members of the college and professional school faculties, selected by the graduate school, should give graduate courses and be responsible for supervision of theses and dissertations, under the direction of the graduate dean and his faculty.

This arrangement would not require separate departments in the graduate school. The three broad fields of knowledge—the humanities, the social sciences, and the natural sciences—should be well represented, but not all departments. The graduate faculty members should be *ex officio* members of their particular college or professional school departments.

If a master's or Ph.D. candidate should apply for work leading to a degree in a department not represented on the graduate faculty, a member of the appropriate undergraduate department could be selected by the dean of the school for service as a part-time graduate faculty member and, in that capacity, would supervise the thesis or dissertation of the candidate. Such an arrangement should insure against the graduate faculty's becoming "isolated or insulated" from the undergraduate faculty. Further insurance would be provided by the faculty committees composed of both undergraduate and graduate faculty members, as suggested in the preceding chapter, and by graduate faculty members' giving undergraduate courses. These arrangements should make for greater unity than now exists between the undergraduate and graduate divisions of the university. They should also enable the graduate dean and his faculty to select the ablest members of the college and professional school departments, regardless of age or rank, to participate in the graduate education program.

CHAPTER 13

Summary and
Program Recommendations

The graduate school currently is the most strategic segment of higher education, and its effectiveness is of great concern to the entire educational system, to our defense effort, and to government, business, and industry, which employ almost one half of all Ph.D. graduates.

The second conclusion is that the graduate school at the present time is the most inefficient and, in some ways, the most ineffective division of the university, as evidenced in the high attrition rate, the lag between the B.A. and the Ph.D., and the great gap between the supply and demand for Ph.D. graduates. The records show that less than 50 per cent of the candidates for the Ph.D. succeed in achieving it, while 85 to 90 per cent of the candidates for the M.D. are successful. Of those who finally achieve the Ph.D., only a minor fraction receive it in three years after the B.A., the time requirement announced in catalogues. The average lag is roughly seven to twelve years, depending upon the subject area of the candidate. The annual production of Ph.D. graduates is less than half the number required, and the demand in the next fifteen years will probably be double that of the present.

The third conclusion is that the *most urgent need* of American education is a thoroughgoing reform of our graduate education program. Piecemeal, halfhearted attacks on the manifold problems outlined in earlier chapters will not suffice. A comprehensive and determined effort to reform the policies and

195

practices of graduate schools will be required. To be specific, I shall list certain of the more significant problem areas involved in the foregoing broad statement.

1. Recruitment of graduate students has been one of the weakest links in the graduate education program. In the main, graduate schools have made no systematic effort to lure the ablest students into advanced work. Recruitment should begin in high school.

2. The college should not only recruit able high school seniors and encourage them early to consider graduate work, but should provide such learning experiences as would fit undergraduates for advanced work. An aggressive graduate faculty which would enlist the cooperation of the college faculty in their recruitment efforts could make a great difference in the number and quality of graduate students.

3. Perhaps the most important single step that could be taken to improve the quality and increase the number of graduate students would be to reorganize procedures so as to give the able student the same kind of assurance that he would get his Ph.D. in three years beyond the B.A., if he did his part, as medical schools give their M.D. candidates. Uncertainty drives away the ablest students. As Jacques Barzun said, "The more vigorous minds seem to turn to the 'sterner and more competitive professions' such as law and medicine, where candidates must march through on schedule, meeting more rigorous and more specific demands."[1]

4. The contention that there is something different about graduate studies that makes it impossible to tell when or whether one can secure a Ph.D. is a rationalization of the results of the laissez-faire attitude of the faculty, or of their poor selection of graduate students, or of the anarchy that prevails in graduate schools.

5. The lack of articulation between undergraduate and graduate education is a basic weakness in our higher education system. In some ways the adjustment of the college graduate to

[1] Quoted by Loren B. Pope, *New York Times*, April 19, 1959.

advanced work is more difficult than that of the high school graduate to college. We have not only one system of higher education but two, the one covering four years and the other theoretically requiring three, but actually in some cases extending over many years.

6. Another facet of the lack of articulation is found in the disparity between the focus of education provided by the graduate schools and that of the college where the Ph.D. graduate is expected to teach. This is blamed by some for the decline of the liberal arts college in recent years and by others for the unwarranted specialization, departmentalization, and fragmentation of knowledge in our colleges and universities.

7. Many complaints have been registered against the graduate schools for failure to recognize their function in the preparation of college teachers. This, in turn, is blamed for the proliferation of courses in the college and for the disintegration of liberal education. There is considerable validity in this indictment. The nature of the research in the humanities and in the social sciences is often unsuited to the needs of future college teachers. More emphasis on the significant ideals and concepts upon which our culture rests is an obvious but frequently unrecognized need. In addition, some broad courses such as *The History of University Education, The Role of Science in the Modern World,* or *The Function of Higher Education in Modern Society,* should be required of those planning to enter college teaching. The Doctor of Philosophy degree for the teacher should be superior in breadth to, and equally as rigorous in its research requirements as, that awarded for scientific or professional investigation. As a means of distinguishing between the two, the abbreviation might be D.Phil. instead of Ph.D.

8. A series of internal graduate school problems relates to the scope and purpose of the qualifying examination for admission to Ph.D. candidacy, the foreign language requirement, the nature and purpose of the dissertation, and the final examination of the candidate after his dissertation has been received and approved. More general questions, such as the amount of course

work that should be required of the Ph.D. candidate, the amount and kind of assistance the student should have in choosing his dissertation topic, and the kind of supervision and guidance that should be given the candidate in his research and writing are still unanswered. The variability between and within universities in these matters makes for confusion.

9. Finally, the proliferation of graduate courses and graduate degrees in American universities is a matter of concern to thoughtful educators. "When seventy-five universities offer 14,732 courses open to graduate students, and when universities award 68 different kinds of doctorates and 150 different master's degrees,"[2] it would appear that the program of American higher learning should be reviewed and scrutinized critically.

The fourth conclusion is that a study of these and other problems is the responsibility of the graduate schools, and that they are not organized or equipped to fulfill this responsibility.

Finally, in view of the acute shortage of teachers, the graduate schools, in cooperation with the colleges, should actively recruit for the teaching profession and should provide special programs designed to exalt the teaching profession, to inform both undergraduate and graduate students about the needs and the rewards of the profession, and, thus, to build greater interest in it. The pregraduates, suggested in Chapter 11, would provide a natural group for such a program, which could be organized and promoted by the pregraduate and graduate committees of the faculty, which are recommended for the development of the three-year master's program.

It is of the utmost importance that we take the long view in planning education for the youth of tomorrow. Discoveries already made and those in the making will probably make life in America in A.D. 2000 as different from that of today as life in 1961 is different from that of 1800. But the college students of this decade will still be active in A.D. 2000, and the elementary school children will be in the prime of life. What should we be

[2] John E. Horner, "A Dangerous Trend in Graduate Education," *The Journal of Higher Education*, XXX, No. 3 (March 1959), p. 168.

giving them as preparation for life at that time? Surely it must be an understanding of the fundamentals of our culture—the concepts and ideals that underlie it; the meaning of science and technology and the changes they impose; the difference between the trivial and the significant, the temporary and the lasting, and a sense of values that will guide them along the high road.

Perhaps this excursion into the future appears to be a detour. What relevance have these considerations in a discussion of graduate education? The tone and quality of the entire educational system is influenced substantially by what goes on in graduate schools, where all college teachers and some public school teachers and administrators receive their preparation. For this reason, the graduate school faculties should be looking ahead, anticipating long-range needs, and reshaping the educational program to meet them.

The principal recommendations embodied in the graduate program are outlined below:

1. Each graduate school should have at least a small full-time faculty responsible to the dean of the school, who would have a budget sufficient not only for his full-time staff but for part-time faculty who might be chosen from other divisions of the university. The full-time status of graduate faculty members should not be interpreted as precluding their teaching undergraduate courses. Indeed, each member should be expected to give at least one semester or year course each year in the college. This plan, coupled with that of having undergraduate faculty members give graduate courses regularly, should assure that there would be no "isolation or insulation" of the graduate faculty.

2. The dean and his full-time colleagues would be responsible for revising the doctoral program to the end that an able student could plan his graduate work with as much certainty of completing it on schedule as the undergraduate or professional student has.

3. Pregraduate programs should be encouraged in the colleges. The graduate school faculty should not only encourage this

development but assist in formulating the curriculum for the pregraduate. Recruitment for the program should begin with high school seniors and continue through the first two years of college. Junior and senior colleges that cooperate in the three-year master's plan could provide additional recruitment services.

4. Requirements for the pregraduate should be more rigorous than for the average upper-class college student and should include a course or two pointing to graduate work and sufficient foreign language instruction to enable the student to pass the examinations required by the graduate school, either in his senior year or in the summer following graduation. Pregraduates should normally be selected from students who are at least in the upper 20 per cent of the class.

5. The pregraduate program should be designed to assist articulation of undergraduate and graduate work. To this end, appropriate research projects should be assigned to junior and senior students, thus developing some capacity for research and acquaintance with its techniques. Other requirements, such as independent reading in preparation for the Ph.D. qualifying examination, might be formulated which would make the transition from college to graduate school smoother and less wasteful of student time.

6. A small committee, or committees,[3] of college faculty members should be appointed to give special attention to the pregraduate group, with a view to making recommendations to graduate faculties where they may apply for admission to graduate schools. Such committees might also devise ways and means of promoting an interest in the teaching profession.

7. A similar committee in the graduate school faculty, giving special attention to those who plan to enter college teaching, could be helpful in strengthening the interest of all graduate students by emphasizing the current and prospective need for college and university teachers.

8. A full-time graduate faculty, devoting major attention to

[3] At least in the larger colleges, it would seem wise to have one committee for the humanities and the social science students and another for those in the natural sciences.

the needs of graduate education, would doubtless find many ways of improving the graduate school curriculum as it relates to those who plan to enter the teaching profession.

9. The three-year master's degree plan should become the gateway to the doctorate. Its main features are early identification of talent, the pregraduate classification, the more rigorous program of studies, the introduction of the university idea of scholarship in the junior year, preparation for the doctor's degree qualifying and foreign language examinations, and fitting the student for achieving the doctorate in two years beyond the master's degree. *It is recommended that this degree be styled the Master of Philosophy (M.Phil.), and that the doctor's degree based on it be known as the Doctor of Philosophy (D.Phil.).* These designations would make it easy to distinguish between those prepared for college teaching (D.Phil.) and the purely scientific or professional doctorates (Ph.D.).

Joint committees of graduate schools and college faculties, focusing attention on the ways and means of recruiting for college and university teaching, might easily be able to create a new climate of opinion in universities respecting the need for teachers and the rewards of college teaching as a career. This should increase materially the number of qualified graduate students and, hence, enable the graduate schools to produce better qualified doctoral candidates for college and university posts in a shorter time and in greater numbers.

Such reforms as are proposed here might be tried out for a five-year period. They cannot take place overnight. Time will be required and perhaps successful experiments to persuade institutions to accept the program. A limited number of universities and colleges might be willing to experiment with a plan involving the principles embodied in the proposals.

Perhaps this should be said: No elements of the scheme proposed are without precedents already in operation in colleges and universities. The only thing new is the application of certain principles to the graduate school. In every instructional division, except the graduate school, the dean has a budget, a faculty, the authority and responsibility within limits to control what goes on, to establish regulations with the help of his faculty, to pass upon the qualifications of its graduates, etc. If the idea of turning the graduate school into a professional school is thought to be inappropriate, it should be remembered that the medieval university, the earliest example of a community of scholars, had as its chief purpose the training of *masters* and *doctors* who were qualified to teach, who had achieved *ius docendi ubique* ("the right to teach anywhere"). In any case, since the graduate school is the only agency our society has for carrying on the purpose of the medieval university—'preparing masters and doctors for teaching'—it must perforce perform this essential function.

"A Future for Graduate Education" was the title of the late Walter Jessup's last annual report as president of the Carnegie Foundation for the Advancement of Teaching. Though written more than fifteen years ago, it is still timely and provocative. I conclude this report on graduate education with the sentiments expressed in the final paragraph of that report:

Before American higher education, and especially graduate education, a new future of achievement is about to open. For that future the prime need is men of vitality, wisdom, and insight, who, whether as teachers or scholars, deans or presidents, shall have the boldness to lay bold plans without recourse to delay and temporizing, and when the moment for action arrives take it and lead their fellows forward. American graduate education must justify by its own reinvigoration the faith which our people has long manifested.[4]

[4] The Carnegie Foundation for the Advancement of Teaching, *Annual Report of the President*, 1943-44.

Bibliography

AMERICAN ASSOCIATION OF COLLEGES FOR TEACHER EDUCATION. *The Doctorate in Education.* Vols. I and II. Washington, D. C., 1960.

AMERICAN COUNCIL ON EDUCATION. *American Universities and Colleges* (8th ed.), 1960.

————. *Graduate Study for Future College Teachers* by Joseph Alexrod. 1959. Report of the Conference on College Teacher Preparation Programs Sponsored by the Committee on College Teaching of the American Council on Education in Washington, D. C., April 30 and May 1, 1958.

————. *Higher Education and National Affairs,* Vol. IX, No. 13, March 1960.

————. *Sponsored Research Policy of Colleges and Universities.* A report of the Committee on Institutional Research Policy. 1954

AMERICAN HOME ECONOMICS ASSOCIATION. *Home Economics-New Directions, A Statement of Philosophy and Objectives.* Prepared by the Committee on Philosophy and Objectives of Home Economics. Washington, D. C., June 1959.

ASSOCIATION OF AMERICAN COLLEGES. *A Guide to Graduate Study.* Washington, D. C., 1957.

BERELSON, BERNARD. *Graduate Education in the United States.* ("The Carnegie Series in American Education.") New York: McGraw-Hill Book Co., Inc., 1960.

————. *Post-Doctoral Work in American Universities.* New York: Bureau of Applied Social Research, Columbia University, October 1960. A report to the A.A.U.

————. "Trends and Choices in Graduate Education." Talk at Amherst, Mass., April 15, 1959.

BOWLES, FRANK H. *Admission to College—A Perspective for the 1960's.* 57th Report of the President, College Entrance Examination Board. 1960.

CARMICHAEL, OLIVER C. *Universities: Commonwealth and American.* A Comparative Study. New York: Harper & Brothers, 1959.

CARNEGIE CORPORATION OF NEW YORK. *Quarterly Report*, Vol. VIII, No. 1, January 1960.

———. *Report of the President and of the Treasurer. 1938.*

CARNEGIE FOUNDATION FOR THE ADVANCEMENT OF TEACHING. *Annual Reports*, 1943-44, 1947-48, 1948-49, 1949-50, 1950-51, 1951-52, 1952-53, 1953-54.

———. *Federal Programs in Higher Education.* (Reprinted from the 1956-1957 *Annual Report*.) *Summary of a Discussion by the Trustees of the Carnegie Foundation for the Advancement of Teaching.*

CORSON, JOHN J., *Governance of Colleges and Universities.* ("The Carnegie Series in American Education.") New York: McGraw-Hill Book Co., Inc., 1960.

DUNBAR, R. E., and BROBERG, J. W. "Graduate Examination Practices at the M.S. and M.A. Levels," *Journal of Chemical Education*, Vol. XXXVII, May 1960, p. 254.

DRESSEL, PAUL L., MAYHEW, LEWIS B., and McGRATH, EARL J. *The Liberal Arts as Viewed by Faculty Members in Professional Schools.* Published for the Institute of Higher Education by the Bureau of Publications, Teachers College, Columbia University, N. Y., 1959.

EDDY, EDWARD DANFORTH. *Colleges for Our Land and Time.* New York: Harper & Brothers, 1957.

Educational Forum, The, Vol. XXV, No. 2, January 1961.

ELDER, J. P. *A Criticism of the Graduate School of Arts and Sciences in Harvard University and Radcliffe College.* From those who took the Ph.D. at these institutions between 1950 and 1954. Spring 1958.

GARDNER, JOHN W. *Excellence.* New York: Harper & Brothers, 1961.

Graduate Instruction and Research. A Report of the President's Task Force of the City College of the College of the City of New York, November 1, 1960.

HANCHER, VIRGIL M. *"The Challenges We Face,"* The Educational Record, January 1959.

INSTITUTE OF INTERNATIONAL EDUCATION ANNUAL REPORT. New York, 1960.

Journal of Higher Education, Vol. XXX, No. 3, March 1959; Vol. XXXI, No. 3, March 1960.

Journal of Proceedings and Addresses. The fifty-ninth annual conference of the Association of American Universities and tenth annual conference of the Association of Graduate Schools, Chicago, Ill., October 1958.

KEEZER, DEXTER M. *Financing Higher Education: 1960-70.* ("The McGraw-Hill Book Company 50th Anniversary Study of the Economics of Higher Education in the United States.") New York: Mc-Graw-Hill Book Co., Inc., 1959.

KNIGHT, DOUGLAS M. Charles A. Quattlebaum, James McCormack, Vincent

A. Fulmer, John A. Perkins, Daniel W. Wood. *The Federal Government and Higher Education.* The American Assembly Columbia University. New Jersey: Prentice-Hall, Inc., 1960.

McCain, James A. "The Expansion of Educational Opportunity in Europe," *Journal of Higher Education,* Vol. XXXI, No. 2, February 1960.

———. "Professors and Students in European Universities," *Journal of Higher Education,* Vol. XXXI, No. 4, April 1960.

McGrath, Earl J. *The Graduate School and the Decline of Liberal Education.*

———. *Liberal Education in the Professions.* New York: Bureau of Publications, Teachers College, Columbia University, 1959. Published for the Institute of Higher Education.

McGrath, Earl J., and Russell, Charles H. *Are Liberal Arts Colleges Becoming Professional Schools?* New York: Bureau of Publications, Teachers College, Columbia University, 1958.

National Academy of Sciences, National Research Council. *Industrial Research Laboratories of the United States* (Publication No. 379) (10th ed.) Washington, D. C., 1956. Compiled by James F. Mauk with the assistance of Harold Peacock and Melvin S. Ruffner, under the direction of Charles I. Campbell.

National Science Foundation. *Directory of Independent Commercial Laboratories Performing Research and Development 1957.* (NSF 57-40) Washington, D. C.: Government Printing Office, 1958.

———. *Funds for Research and Development in Industry 1957.* (NSF 60-49, "Surveys of Science Resources Series") Washington, D. C.: Government Printing Office, 1960.

———. *The Long-Range Demand for Scientific and Technical Personnel— A Methodological Study.* Prepared by the U. S. Dept. of Labor, Bureau of Labor Statistics. Preliminary draft.

———. *Reviews of Data on Research & Development.* (NSF 59-65) Washington, D. C.: Government Printing Office, 1959.

———. *Reviews of Data on Research & Development.* (NSF 60-35, No. 20) Washington, D. C.: Government Printing Office, 1960.

———. *Science and Engineering in American Industry.* (NSF 56-16). Final Report on a 1953-1954 Survey. U. S. Dept. of Labor, Bureau of Labor Statistics, 1956.

———. *Science and Engineering in American Industry.* (NSF 59-50) Report on a 1956 Survey. U. S. Dept. of Labor, Bureau of Labor Statistics. Washington, D. C.: Government Printing Office, 1959.

———. *The Science Doctorates of 1957 and 1958, their Numbers, Backgrounds, and Employment.* By Lindsey R. Harmon. Scientific Manpower Report, March 17, 1959. Office of Scientific Personnel, National Academy of Sciences, National Research Council, Washington, D. C.

——. *Scientific and Technical Personnel in American Industry.* (NSF 60-62) Report on a 1959 Survey. Prepared by the U. S. Dept. of Labor, Bureau of Labor Statistics. Washington, D. C.: Government Printing Office, 1960.

NATIONAL EDUCATION ASSOCIATION. *Research Bulletin,* Vol. XXXVIII, No. 2., May 1960.

——. *Teacher Supply and Demand in Colleges and Universities, 1955-56 and 1956-57.* A study conducted by the Research Division of the N.E.A. with financial assistance from the Fund for the Advancement of Education. Washington, D. C.

——. *Teacher Supply and Demand in Universities, Colleges, and Junior Colleges, 1957-58 and 1958-59.* (Higher Education Series, 1959-R10). A study conducted by the Research Division of the N.E.A. with financial assistance from the Fund for the Advancement of Education. Washington, D. C., 1959.

NEW ENGLAND BOARD OF HIGHER EDUCATION. *Faculty Preparation and Orientation.* Ed. JOHN W. GUSTAD. Proceedings of a Regional Conference, Boston, Mass., February 11-12, 1960.

——. *Faculty Supply, Demand and Recruitment.* Ed. JOHN W. GUSTAD. Proceedings of a Regional Conference, Boston, Mass., November 5-7, 1959.

NEW YORK, STATE UNIVERSITY OF. *Meeting the Increasing Demand for Higher Education in New York State.* A Report to the Governor and the Board of Regents by the Committee on Higher Education—MARION B. FOLSOM, JOHN W. GARDNER, and HENRY T. HEALD, chairman. Director of Studies, SIDNEY G. TICKTON. November 1960.

POPE, LOREN B. "Education in Review—Graduate Schools Concerned by Failure to Produce enough Ph.D.'s Yearly," *New York Times,* April 19, 1959.

PRESIDENT'S COMMITTEE ON EDUCATION BEYOND THE HIGH SCHOOL. *Second Report to the President.* Washington, D. C.: Government Printing Office, July 1957.

PRESIDENT'S SCIENCE ADVISORY COMMITTEE. *Strengthening American Science.* Washington, D. C.: Government Printing Office, December 1958.

ROCKEFELLER BROTHERS FUND. *The Power of the Democratic Idea.* ("Special Studies Project Report VI.") Garden City, N. Y.: Doubleday & Co., Inc., 1960.

ROSENHAUPT, HANS, assisted by CHINLUND, THOMAS J. *Graduate Students Experience at Columbia University, 1940-1956.* New York: Columbia University Press, 1958.

ROSS, MURRAY G. "Education in the U.S.S.R." *Toronto Daily Star,* 1958.

SOUTHERN FELLOWSHIPS FUND. *Doctoral Dissertations by 87 Recipients of Fellowship Grants from the Southern Fellowships Fund,* by ROBERT M. LESTER. Chapel Hill, N. C., November 1960.

―――. *Doctoral Dissertations by 150 Recipients of Fellowship Grants from the Southern Fellowship Fund, 1955-58,* by ROBERT M. LESTER. Chapel Hill, N. C.

―――. Table I, "Ph.D. Degrees Conferred by Southern Universities, 1948-55"; Table II, "Ph.D. Degrees in Humanities Conferred by Southern Universities, 1948-55, by Fields of Interest"; Table III, "Ph.D. Degrees in Humanities Conferred by Non-Southern Universities." Chapel Hill, N. C., September 3, 1958.

SOUTHERN REGIONAL EDUCATION BOARD.
Prospectus for a Study of Factors Affecting the Length of Doctoral Programs. April 3, 1959.
Financing Higher Education, Numbers 1-7.
Regional Action, Vol. II, No. 2, June, 1960.
The Career Decisions of College Teachers ("SREB Research Monograph Series," No. 2.), by John W. Gustad, Atlanta 13, Ga., November 1960. A cooperative research project sponsored jointly by the SREB and University of Maryland.

STROTHMANN, F. W. *The Graduate School Today and Tomorrow.* N. Y.: Fund for the Advancement of Education, 1955.

Superior Student, The, Vol. III, No. 6, October 1960. (University of Colorado, Boulder, Colo.).

TAYLOR, HUGH. *Graduate Education at Princeton, 1945 to 1958.*

TEPS Newsletter, Vol. III, No. 3, February 1960. (National Commission on Teacher Education and Professional Standards, National Education Association of the United States, Washington, D. C.)

U. S. DEPARTMENT OF HEALTH, EDUCATION, AND WELFARE, OFFICE OF EDUCATION. *The Gifted Student.* (OE-35016, Cooperative Research Monograph No. 2) Washington, D. C.: Government Printing Office, 1960.

―――. *Resident, Extension, and Other Enrollments in Institutions of Higher Education, First Term 1957-58,* by HAZEL C. POOLE, under the general direction of MABEL C. RICE. (Circular No. 593.) Washington, D. C.: Government Printing Office, 1959.

―――. *A Statistical Comparison of Graduate Degrees Awarded by Members of the Association of Graduate Schools and by all U. S. Universities, 1957-58,* by JOHN L. CHASE, JAMES H. BLESSING, and GRANDIS L. KING. (OE-54011.) Washington, D. C., September 1960.

―――. *Statistics of Land-Grant Colleges and Universities, Year ended June 30, 1958,* by GEORGE LIND and MABEL C. RICE. (Circular No. 612.) Washington, D. C.: Government Printing Office, 1960.

————. *Survey of State Legislation Relating to Higher Education, July 1, 1958, to December 31, 1959,* by ERNEST V. HOLLIS, WILLIAM G. LAND, and S. V. MARTORANA. (Circular No. 618.) Washington, D. C.: Government Printing Office, 1960.

————. *State Boards Responsible for Higher Education,* by S. V. MARTORANA and ERNEST V. HOLLIS. (Circular No. 619.) Washington, D.C.: Government Printing Office, 1960.

UNIVERSITY MICROFILMS, INC. *Dissertation Abstracts,* Vol. XXI, No. 1. Ann Arbor, Mich., 1960.

INDEX

209